Praise For

EDWARD FEUZ JR

A STORY OF ENCHANTMENT

"It's rare to come across an author whose formative years climbing in the Rockies reach back to, and intersect with, the life of an iconic Swiss mountain guide who was in the employ of the Canadian Pacific Railway. Donna Stephen and her adventuresome family were introduced to the wilds of the Canadian cordillera by none other than Edward Feuz Jr., who taught them how to pace themselves in order to properly absorb a love for the mountains. Rich in immigrant Swiss guide history, this book paints a 3D picture of what the guides and their guests sought, equipped with the most basic of climbing aids, decades before the advent of bear spray and the lottery system required to visit these now crowded destinations."

—PAT MORROW, adventure photographer, filmmaker, author of *Beyond Everest: Quest for the Seven Summits* and *Searching For Tao Canyon*

"The Swiss guides made mountaineering a profession and turned Canada into an alpine nation. Then they taught us to ski, which made the Canadian winter ours. A story of enchantment indeed!"

—ROBERT WILLIAM SANDFORD, author of *The Columbia Icefield — 3rd Edition* and *Our Vanishing Glaciers: The Snows of Yesteryear and the Future Climate of the Mountain West*

EDWARD FEUZ JR.

EDWARD FEUZ JR.

A STORY OF ENCHANTMENT

D. L. STEPHEN

RMB

In memory of Edward.
You live in our hearts.

For Pat,
with all my love and gratitude.

And to Cindy,
my favourite climbing partner.

For information on purchasing bulk quantities of this book, or to obtain media excerpts or invite the author to speak at an event, please visit rmbooks.com and select the "Contact" tab.

RMB | Rocky Mountain Books Ltd.
rmbooks.com
@rmbooks
facebook.com/rmbooks

Cataloguing data available from Library and Archives Canada
ISBN 9781771605090 (softcover)
ISBN 9781771605106 (electronic)

Printed and bound in Canada

We would like to also take this opportunity to acknowledge the traditional territories upon which we live and work. In Calgary, Alberta, we acknowledge the Niitsítapi (Blackfoot) and the people of the Treaty 7 region in Southern Alberta, which includes the Siksika, the Piikuni, the Kainai, the Tsuut'ina, and the Stoney Nakoda First Nations, including Chiniki, Bearpaw, and Wesley First Nations. The City of Calgary is also home to Métis Nation of Alberta, Region III. In Victoria, British Columbia, we acknowledge the traditional territories of the Lkwungen (Esquimalt and Songhees), Malahat, Pacheedaht, Scia'new, T'Sou-ke, and W̱SÁNEĆ (Pauquachin, Tsartlip, Tsawout, Tseycum) peoples.

We acknowledge the financial support of the Government of Canada through the Canada Book Fund and the Canada Council for the Arts, and of the province of British Columbia through the British Columbia Arts Council and the Book Publishing Tax Credit.

Canada Council Conseil des Arts
for the Arts du Canada

BRITISH COLUMBIA
ARTS COUNCIL
An agency of the Province of British Columbia

Most happenings are beyond expression;
they exist where a word has never intruded.

— RAINER MARIA RILKE

The love of the mountains is a thing
that is very hard to explain.

— EDWARD FEUZ

CONTENTS

PREFACE

Mountains were in Edward's genetic makeup. They were all around him. They were in the air he breathed. They were an irresistible, omnipresent force. Not surprisingly, given the various circumstances in his life, he became a mountain guide. He made more first ascents of Canadian mountains than any of his peers. If achievements are a measure of a life, he was successful. He was also famous. But when asked if he knew he had been making history, he laughed and said, "I never thought about it." The real appeal of Edward's story is more intangible. If it could be summarized in one word, that word would be *passion*.

Whether we march solidly along on a well-defined path in life or simply meander, we are fortunate when our journeys lead us to encounters with people whose luminosity is of a special intensity. Edward Feuz Jr. was one such person. Many counted themselves fortunate to have met him.

This story has a memoir component, but it is not about me or my family. We are vehicles to convey the enchantment that hundreds before us felt, and I am just the narrator. It is Edward who leads us through the forest and onto the mountain top.

ACKNOWLEDGEMENTS

I owe a debt of gratitude to the employees, interns and volunteers at the Whyte Museum of the Canadian Rockies. In particular, I wish to thank Elizabeth Kundert-Cameron and Lena Goon for sharing their truly encyclopedic knowledge, and also for their enthusiastic support of this project. My sincere thanks to Lindsay Stokalko for scanning images and for her assistance in difficult times. In addition to the Whyte Museum, I wish to thank the City of Vancouver Archives (for producing a high-quality scan of one of their images), as well as Panda Lab in Seattle and ABL Imaging in Calgary for their excellent work with privately held materials. A special thanks is owed to Constantinos Costoulas at Resolve Photo for his patience and expert eye in preparing images for printing.

Various members of the Feuz clan were very generous in sharing their memories and perspectives with me. The late Jean Vaughan was invaluable for providing details of family life at Edelweiss Village and in sharing impressions of her uncle Edward. Her brother, the late Syd Feuz, was also happy to share childhood memories with me, as was their cousin, Alice Pollard. Karen Smedley kindly gave me access to audio materials she collected in talks with her great-uncle Edward.

Rudi Gertsch provided me with some charming anecdotes. I wish to thank Sepp Renner for reading the final chapter of the manuscript and for providing me with some valuable insights. *Îsniyes* to Îyârhe Nakoda elder Helmer Twoyoungmen, who reviewed my necessarily brief remarks on the extremely complex subject of the impact of the treaties and of the Canadian Pacific Railway on Indigenous peoples.

Special thanks to Susan Andrews, who read an early draft and has been enormously helpful and supportive in innumerable ways throughout this project and far beyond.

I would further like to thank RMB publisher Don Gorman for taking a chance on a first-time author. Also my editor, Joe Wilderson, not only for his attention to detail but also for his perspicacity in helping me create the best manuscript possible.

Many others have encouraged me on this journey and offered practical advice. Most particularly I am very grateful to my biggest supporter, my mother, Pat Stephen, for all her work on the manuscript, and to Cindy Schroeder, who is really my co-narrator. Last but certainly not least, my deepest gratitude to Jim Sykes for his support, his almost infinite patience throughout this long project, for reading various sections, and for chuckling in all the right places.

Finally, I wish to acknowledge that this story takes place on the traditional territories of Indigenous peoples throughout the Canadian Rockies, in the Columbia River Valley and throughout the Columbia Mountains.

CHAPTER 1

PILGRIMS

Walking single file, they wend their way from switchback to switchback, leaving the small blue alpine lake behind them. The leader of this ragtag assembly lets out a *whoa-ho-ho-ho*. It is more like a bellow than a yodel, and the others are startled by the suddenness of it. In stark contrast to his charges, he is dressed rather nattily. His knickerbocker trousers are brown woollen tweed, falling barely below his knees. The long, handmade woollen socks he is wearing are pulled up over the hems of the knickers and then folded back down again to form a four-inch band over each knee. Slung over his canvas rucksack is a matching button-up suit jacket, the arms of which are tucked through the straps of his rucksack. Just below the lapel of this jacket is a large, oval-shaped badge signifying his craft. The sleeves of his plaid shirt are pushed up, revealing thick forearms and wrists. In one hand is an ice axe. On his head is a heather-coloured alpine hat; on his feet are stout leather over-the-ankle boots with Vibram soles, a concession to modernity. The second in line carries a coiled rope across one of her shoulders.

The leader walks as he always does uphill: with slow, rhythmic, machine-like precision, upward and upward until he reaches his goal. Soon, glaciated peaks come into view across the valley and there are gasps of delight at this familiar sight. The group heads west into a straggly stand of trees. He stops to point out that mountain goats have been there. They pick some of the evidence of this from a branch and thrill to the feel of the coarse white hair as they roll it between their fingers.

They are roped together now, and the terrain is becoming rocky and steeper. The leader stops again momentarily and smiles, gesturing to a patch of moss campion. This small pink flower – a symbol of survival in high places – is his favourite. Mostly they travel together but then later move out to the steeper north side of the mountain, where they climb singly using feet and hands. He stands above an overhanging bit of rock, the rope taut in his hands, conveying the strength and confidence to haul up anyone who falters. Scampering with confidence earns a smile and a "very good." Eventually there is no more climbing to do; the party has attained the summit of the Devils Thumb, led by octogenarian Edward Feuz Jr., Swiss guide.

CHAPTER 2

EDWARD

Called the patriarch of North American alpinism and "justly revered as one of great names in all mountaineering,"[1] he became the grand old man of the mountains – the embodiment of all the glamour, adventure and romance of a bygone era. Although he lived well into his 97th year, it was not mere longevity that made Edward's fame.

A letter delivered to him early in his career typified his pre-eminence. Postmarked from Europe, it was addressed simply:

Edward Feuz
Canada

Much to Edward's own amazement, the letter somehow found its way to him – across the sea and then along the rails all the way from eastern Canada to an obscure little town in British Columbia. The identity of the writer and the content of the message have been lost to time, but although the letter disappeared, its envelope endured for several decades, occasionally being brought out by Edward's wife for the amusement of friends.

Edward was the head guide at the centre of the

Canadian mountain universe, Lake Louise. He climbed hundreds of mountains – indeed, most of the major peaks in the Rocky and Selkirk mountains – repeating some ascents dozens of times or even more. He was mentioned in newspaper articles. His accomplishments were discussed in magazines, books and journals. He received honours, became the subject of art and film and was even immortalized in *Ripley's Believe It or Not*. By the end of his career he had made over one hundred first ascents of mountains (more than any of his peers), set a standard for excellence, and trained a new generation of guides and climbers. More importantly, he was a well-loved and respected guide, admired by many as "…the finest guide in the Canadian Rockies…"[2]

Edward was a relatively short fellow, extraordinarily strong, who had a solid, rooted presence but also possessed boundless energy. He spoke in a pleasingly resonant, yet powerful – one could say booming – voice, with a strong *Schweizerdeutsch** accent. Although physical beauty is a subjective matter, there could be no dispute that he was a "head-turner." Even at age 65 he had a stunningly handsome face, a full head of hair, and blue eyes with a confident, direct gaze that could be positively unsettling. A charming little smile frequently formed at the corners of his mouth, and when that happened his eyes sparkled with a seductive intensity.

If he could seem frustratingly rigid in his approach to

---

* The standard German word referring to the Swiss German dialects, of which there are many. Swiss German speakers learn standard German in school but speak their dialect at home.

tasks, this was because he set extremely high standards and expectations for himself and thereby for others. For Edward, whether amongst the peaks or at home, there was a clearly defined right way to do things – and by implication, a wrong way. And he was not shy about sharing what to him were obvious imperatives. Although resolute in his opinions, he could (and did) change his stance and behaviour when presented with a good argument. If he still did not agree with a point of view, he would end a discussion, civilly, with, "Well, you may be right." Of course, the latent sentiment was "but I don't think so."

Like all natural leaders, Edward did not make his way in the world by being wishy-washy or indecisive. Such resolve could at times produce an initial impression of gruffness, while an aloofness that some saw in him was probably reflective of Swiss reserve. Although some people could find Edward's more forthright characteristics intimidating, beneath the superficialities beat a tender and generous heart. Most people who actually knew him remember him for his enthusiasm, cheerful disposition and outsized personality. Although not chatty, Edward was essentially of a gregarious nature, with a quick wit and a mischievous sense of humour. He had an inherent understanding of people and was sensitive to their motives. One could find him discreetly scanning his environment for subtle non-verbal cues and silently taking note.

Like many of his generation, he was an engaging storyteller, a skill which was enhanced by an impressive memory for mountain minutiae such as the exact topography of a particular area; where water was to be found; what qualities the rock of a particular mountain had and what challenges were to be encountered there. When making an emphatic point, he would remove the omnipresent pipe from his mouth. Then, holding it in his right hand and leaning forward for a pause in the narrative, he very clearly communicated 'listen carefully; this is the crux of the matter.'

A complete mountain man, Edward could paddle a canoe and propel himself through woods and over snowy passes on snowshoes and skis. He pulled his children to school on a toboggan he had made with his own hands. He even made an alpenhorn (for decidedly Swiss reasons) and was skilled enough on steel blades to win an ice-dancing contest. Having a good eye for composition, he enjoyed photography and took his 35-millimetre camera everywhere for snapping up the moment. Who knows, he thought, there might be a perfect cluster of delicate alpine flowers around the next corner, just waiting for posterity. Edward knew that these micro-experiences in life are the emotionally charged events tucked away in the recesses of our brains that bring back intensely vivid flashes of memory.

Edward lived a long and satisfying life as a denizen of the mountains and never grew tired of high places. For all the years he lived, the mountains were like his friends, and each familiar visage made his spirits soar. He could sit and gaze at them for hours, knowing, as all mountain people do, that mountains (even in their individuality) are constantly changing. Sometimes they appear with crystalline clarity and sometimes they are obscured.

Rock mutates in colour and texture; snow and ice can look flat and dreary, sparkling, or dramatic with dark sapphire contrasts. The magic of *Alpenglühen*, alpenglow, can paint mountains deep rose; the darkness of evening turns them to charcoal silhouettes. Like people, mountains have their moods and can be welcoming, foreboding or frustratingly ambiguous. Each encounter with them can stir different emotions and different expectations, and create wholly different experiences when we are amongst them.

Throughout human history mountains have inspired. They have served as symbols for the divine, for the forbidden and the ineffable, and conversely for aspirations of achievement and conquest. Those with European heritages hold in their dim collective memories the view of mountains as sacred and/or fearsome – the high, remote and awe-filled dwelling places of gods and spirits. Some Indigenous peoples today still hold views of mountains, sometimes specific ones, as especially spiritually potent and sacred places.

For Edward, climbing and living amongst mountains was more than an accumulation of summits, and he held a dim view of climbing as conquest. Thus, it comes as no surprise that he did not share A.O. Wheeler's* view that

* A.O. Wheeler (1860–1945) was an Irish Canadian land surveyor who worked as a technical officer of the Department of the Interior, mapping the Selkirk Range. Results were published in a book of the same name; a second volume comprised beautiful sketches, sketch maps and topographical maps of the area. Among other accomplishments, he also worked on the BC/Alberta boundary survey and co-founded the Alpine Club of Canada.

the activity was a simile for warfare: "It is akin to victory on the field of battle. There is little doubt that the feeling of conquest is the true secret of the intense attraction of mountain climbing."[3]

Mountain climbing for Edward was not a symbol or an allegory about life. It *was* life. From his point of view, it was life lived in the best of all possible experiential ways. As Rilke might remark, it was a way beyond words. Being wholly in the mountains and attuned to everything around him generated in him a sense of respect, even awe at times. He also knew there is something inherently gratifying in the sheer physicality of coming to an actual fork in the trail and taking the higher path, in reaching a rock wall and climbing it. And that our feelings upon reaching the summit reflect the indescribable primal joy of travelling on our own feet, and in our own natural environment, to an obvious conclusion: no more incline. Certainly, mountains are "there," as George Mallory apparently once quipped – explaining why people climb, to a newspaper reporter who was no doubt annoying – but maybe some of us climb them, in part, simply because of *what we all are*: creatures capable of experiencing exhilaration.

Although Edward's attitude toward mountains was thoroughly monomaniacal – the world could be grouped into two types of people: climbers and non-climbers – it was pleasingly so. His own identity was first, foremost and always, that of a mountain guide – a *Swiss* mountain guide.

CHAPTER 3

HOW IT ALL BEGAN

Edward Feuz Jr., the eldest child of a mountain guide, was born on November 27, 1884, in the *Berner Oberland* of Switzerland, an environment of wide valleys and lakes, expansive high meadows, cascading waterfalls and towering, glaciated peaks with such famous names as Eiger, Mönch and Jungfrau. The residents spoke, as they do to this day, Swiss German, charming dialects so distinct that they are virtually unintelligible to those who only understand ordinary German.

Interlaken, where Edward grew up, had been a tourist destination long before his time. The German literary celebrity Johann Wolfgang von Goethe had visited in the 18th century. Steamships ferried passengers on the adjacent lakes of Thun and Brienz beginning in the 1830s, and by the mid-nineteenth century, tourists drawn to Interlaken included Lord Byron, Felix Mendelssohn, Count Dmitri Tolstoy and Mark Twain.

As a self-described *Lausbub* (a fun-loving rascal) the young Edward, constantly in trouble for assorted misdemeanours, received repeated thrashings from his beleaguered mother, Susanna, a small woman who eventually had seven other children to contend with.* Edward's biggest offence seems to have been making, as he put it, "loud noises" – achieved with a little gunpowder in a metal pipe – behind the Jungfraublick Hotel. No random noisemaking for this lad. He chose his opportunities carefully in order to maximize the effect. Imagine a wedding party and all their guests revelling in happiness on a perfect summer afternoon... But even with careful planning, not all of his projects were successful. One backfired, literally, creating the most alarming looking "speckles," as Edward called them. His condition, having gunpowder particles embedded all over his face, necessitated being hauled off to the doctor by his frantic mother. The physician calmly picked out all of the ugly particles, and Edward, who emerged without any lasting physical reminders of the incident, was a lucky boy. However, his family did not have much wherewithal, and the costly aftermath of this particular adventure did not especially endear him to his parents.

Edward's other occupation as a young boy, participation in an "Indian gang," also held the potential for bodily harm, as the sole purpose was to dress up in feathers and fight the Indian gang across the valley. Although purportedly holding an excellent record for success, Edward's

* Susanna Feuz (1857–1948) was the daughter of Johannes Feuz and Maria Saltermann. She had 10 children: Eduard (b. 1884); Emil (b. 1886); Ida (b. 1887); Ernst (b. 1889); Ida Emma (1890); Frieda (b. 1892); Walter (b. 1894); Alfred (b. 1895); Clara (b. 1897) and Werner (b. 1898). Ida and Alfred did not survive. See https://ancestors.familysearch.org/en/LCFS-5WH/susanna-feuz-1857-1948; accessed 2021-03-15.

gang was defeated one year when their rivals raided the club's "secret" cave headquarters and made off with all their wooden hatchets and other homemade armaments. The miscellaneous bloodletting that resulted from such clashes was borne stoically by most combatants, and the bashings with wooden hatchets were never significant enough to require serious medical intervention.

Despite his juvenile crimes and mischievous nature, Edward was also a sensitive lad who did make efforts toward amends. On one such day he went up onto the *Schacht Platte*, a ridge where he knew he could pick hazelnuts for his mother. After gathering a large sack of the nuts, he happened upon "some lovely flowers," and was inspired to also bring home a bouquet. While still bending down, flowers in hand, he was besieged by a swarm of what looked like large, black flies. Swinging his alpenstock to brush them away, he quickly realized they were not flies. In torment, with the "flies" in pursuit, he ran back downhill as fast as he could. Flinging open the door of his house, he threw in the sack of hazelnuts, along with the now sad-looking flowers, before rushing out to immerse his swelling head in the fountain. "I was trying to do a good thing for mother," he lamented, but the net effect, another thrashing, was not the outcome he had envisioned.

Growing up in a vertical environment, he had only to cross the street from his house to climb cliffs, which of course he did. Cliff climbing was a semi-sanctioned activity when in the guise of collecting firewood for his mother, but it was still potentially dangerous. As the eldest child, Edward had extra responsibilities in the household. Collecting firewood was far preferable to his other chores – scrubbing the porch or polishing the woodwork – but he was also aware that his paternal grandfather had died while engaged in the mundane task of collecting wood for the hearth. Green trees could not be cut, but deadwood was fair game. As Edward gained experience, his daring steadily increased to the point of lowering himself on a rope over cliffs which were too steep to climb down. "Trees," he said, "were growing in the ugliest places you could imagine."

In one such ugly place, he had come down a cliff (probably just using his hands to hold the rope) to a little ledge he could stand on in order to cut the tree. But as the tree began to fall, one its branches swiped him off balance and he started sliding off the ledge. With his legs already moving over the edge, he clawed out blindly and somehow caught hold of a little branch not much bigger than a finger. Fortunately the branch was well attached to a solidly rooted tree and it saved his life. Edward admitted that the incident scared him, but he also professed, "That's how you get to be a good guide... When you have a slip or two, then you get wise; then you are more careful."

Beginning at about age 10, and continuing for several years, Edward spent six weeks each summer with his maternal grandparents in Gsteigwiler, where he had been born. His grandfather, who had two or three cows and therefore was considered fairly well off, worked principally as a *Stehauer* (a stonemason) and fashioned such things as granite fountains which were shipped to locations all over Switzerland. "We had a grand time there [in Gsteigwiler]," Edward reminisced enthusiastically, but there could not have been much time to be a *Lausbub*. He and his cousin were goatherds and charged with the care of 80 to 100 animals. The boys, who slept under blankets in the hayloft, took the goats up into the high meadows each morning to graze. For an hour or two the goatherders could do as they pleased, and spent most of their free time climbing cliffs. It was an idyllic arrangement for an active young boy enamoured of climbing.

When it was time to come down off the cliffs and leave the upper valley, the boys summoned the goats by sounding little horns. For the most part the goats were co-operative, as they "did not have to shove them much." However, there was "a real devil" amidst the group, a billy, who butted them repeatedly and tried to eat their food. This obnoxious fellow was so persistent that the boys were forced to climb trees, with bread and cheese stuffed into their pockets, in order to eat their lunches in peace.

In the evening, wooden vessels filled with milk were delivered to each goat's owner in the village below. For entertainment after their chores, the boys challenged the village lads to bouts of *Schwingen*, or Swiss wrestling. With both combatants dressed in loose canvas shorts, the aim, Edward explained, was to get a grip on the other fellow's shorts and "swing" him onto his back.

Also when Edward was about 10, his father took him on his first real mountain climb, up the Tschingelhorn – a 3562-metre peak on the boundary between the cantons of Bern and Valois – a picturesque, glaciated mountain which Edward described as "easy."

When he was only 12 he climbed the massive Jungfrau by the hardest route of the time, and the achievement was memorialized with an article – and his photograph – in the newspaper. Already he was gaining fame, but he had some lessons to learn. When the climbers came to a large crevasse, his father and his client crossed over it easily, but Edward, frightened at the sight of a yawning gap before him, hesitated. Demonstrating little sympathy for his son's anxiety, Edward senior gave a strong tug on the rope, which pulled the young Edward right off his feet. Much to his distress, in this instant he had lost his grip on his alpenstock, and one does not drop one's alpenstock no matter what the circumstances. As he landed on his midsection with a thump at the far edge of the crevasse, his legs dangling, he glanced back to see his alpenstock "going like a streak down the mountain." Nevertheless, he got to his feet and managed the rest of the climb without any difficulty, his fear forgotten.

The ascent of the Jungfrau began a truly serious passion for climbing, a passion which would eventually become his career, but such a career was not easily won, at least not initially. Edward senior had other plans for his eldest son. He was to go into the hotel business and hopefully work his way up into management or perhaps even become a proprietor. But first, Feuz reasoned, the boy must learn French. And so, after leaving school, the still adolescent Edward took his first real train journey, to Lausanne. His mother had fashioned a cross out of twigs for his hat.

This way, she had explained, his new employer would be able to recognize him. Although he would have preferred flowers as a motif, he dutifully attached the cross to his hat as soon as he arrived at the train station.

Edward had never been in a big city and Lausanne certainly felt like one to him. On the platform, a tall, strong-looking man stood waiting. Accompanying the taciturn stranger to a small restaurant for a meagre bowl of soup, Edward then rode in a horse-drawn cart to his new home. Pangs of homesickness were already washing over him. Not only was the farm a long way from home, it was surrounded by nothing but rolling hills.

Homesickness, or *Heimweh*, first described in the 1600s, was thought to be a disease specific to the Swiss. A cluster of somatic symptoms, including fever and irregular heartbeat, accompanied this type of melancholy. Mountain dwellers who descended to lower altitudes were particularly vulnerable, it was speculated, due to thickening of the blood.[4] The fictional Heidi, an "unspoiled child of nature" removed from the mountains by force, was a prototypical Swiss sufferer.[5] No doubt Edward had a serious case of *Heimweh*, but he loathed his new situation in life for more than what he felt was its bland geography.

He had a job now, working from dawn until as late as midnight. His primary task was to cut sheaves of wheat by hand. Making the sheaves "stand" properly was not an easy thing to do, especially for a novice. When Edward's initial efforts slumped to the ground (surely not unexpectedly) the farmer was abusive in his displeasure.

Charged also with milking cows and tending horses, Edward found it difficult to fathom how his thralldom, with only farm animals for company, was going to teach him any French.

His father, who came to check on him in the autumn, realized he was being ill used and urged the young Edward to come home. Despondent, Edward explained that he had given his word to remain for one year. To his generation this was an inviolable contract. Moreover, he had signed a written contract as well. He could not leave, and so he stuck it out, lonely and miserable for an entire year, and did not learn much French. Familial ambitions for the young Edward's hotel management career ended with the failed francophone project.

Gratefully escaping mere hills and fields, and returning to his familiar cliffs and glaciers, Edward could not have known that his whole future would nevertheless be shaped by an association with hotels. In the meantime, he obtained his porter's licence, beginning his apprenticeship as a guide, and climbed like a young man obsessed.

Across the sea, the Dominion of Canada had been in existence for a mere 19 years at Edward's birth, the British North America Act having been pushed through the British Parliament on July 1, 1867. Edward was not quite one year old when, in 1885, "the last spike" was driven "among the shrouded mountains in a damp clearing bearing a strange Gaelic name" – Craigellachie[6] The building of this railway was a dramatic and nearly insane national ambition. In a promise to the colonists of British Columbia by Sir John A. Macdonald, Canada's first prime minister, over five thousand miles of track was laid connecting the land from the Atlantic to Pacific oceans, in only four years and six months. The most difficult parts of the task – and it is almost trite to say "difficult" – were the various routes through the mountains, which came at a terrific financial and human cost. The most treacherous portion of the route was through the Selkirk Mountains, specifically through Rogers Pass, a completely isolated and wild place which would become Edward's home in Canada.

Canadian historian Pierre Berton recounted that workers were terrified at the prospect of the Rogers Pass portion of the project, which was not surprising. One RCMP officer attempting to ride over the pass in February 1885 was said to have had to give up and walk the last 15 miles (about 24 kilometres). At the pass he found massive avalanche paths with ice as much as 50 feet (more than 15 metres) thick. Railway workers and their supplies were repeatedly wiped out in slides, and even when all the track was finally laid, huge sections of it were swept away in the first winter. Finally, at great expense, 10 kilometres of snow sheds were built, but even these were ineffective against avalanches, as the crashing of a 10-ton boulder through the roof of one of these sheds demonstrated.[7] However, the job was technically completed and soon the Canadian Pacific Railway's (CPR) steam engines, pulling their wooden cars, would begin making regular trips through the Canadian mountains.[8]

The reigning monarch at the time of this feat was Queen Victoria. The sun was not yet setting on the British Empire, and the Dominion of Canada was very much a part of that. The completion of the trans-Canadian railway was considered a glorious nation-building accomplishment, but there is a very unpleasant subtext to the story.

When Macdonald made his promise to the colonists of British Columbia to build a railroad, he actually had no right to do so. Huge expanses of land through which the train would travel were in the territories of peoples whose rights were protected by Royal Proclamation. This meant there was tremendous pressure for Her Majesty's representatives to sign treaties with these peoples, as this was the only means by which conditions of the Proclamation could be altered. To complicate matters, many Indigenous people believed that the written documents they were encouraged to sign were simply peace treaties. They were not.[9] The specific intent of them was to extinguish Indigenous rights – most importantly by ceding land in traditional territories – so as to not impede the national agenda, which included the building of the railway and other "white progress."[10] The consequences of treaties, along with subsequent government actions and policies, were catastrophic to First Nations, and their adverse effects continue to cause challenges and sorrows which ripple down to the present day.

Historian H.A. Dempsey wrote that the Indigenous leaders had been worried that the advent of the railway would bring enough white people to outnumber them, with less than pleasant results. He quoted the great Cree leader Poundmaker as having said in 1882, "… the railway will be close to us, the whites will fill the country and they will dictate to us as they please. It is useless to dream that we can frighten them; that time has past."[11] Sadly, Poundmaker's fears were not unfounded. The railroad also caused grassfires. Game animals were frightened away, horses were frequently killed and the buffalo quickly disappeared, causing starvation for many.

Despite this dismal context, it was an Îyârhe Nakoda (Stoney) man, Edwin, who led the first non-Aboriginal, Tom Wilson, to the lake of the little fishes in 1882 and told him of the Goats' Looking Glass.[12] And, the special places of exquisite beauty Tom Wilson had been shown – now called Lake Louise and Lake Agnes – eventually were incorporated into Banff National Park and today are part of a UNESCO World Heritage Site.

In theory the idea of protecting special places seems a good one, although the initial motives were not so "pure," as one would have to ask what was protected and for whom.* The establishment of the park reserved resource extraction for only a few, and also ended access to traditional hunting grounds for the Îyârhe Nakoda and other Indigenous peoples, who, at the time of the treaties, certainly would never have knowingly agreed to restricting their usage of traditional land in this or any other way.

Edward's attitude toward Indigenous peoples was positive but rooted in his childhood "Indian gang" days, so his knowledge was fairly abstract. "I liked Indians,

---

* Late in life Edward thought there should be even more national parks in the mountainous regions of Canada; that harvesting of trees and mineral extraction should no longer be allowed as they had been in the past; and that the number of roads and man-made structures should be limited.

yes, but I never met them outside" – he means in the woods. "There were no Indians," he said, "just white people."[13] What happened to the Indigenous people, whose environment this had been, may not have filtered into his consciousness, just as it probably had not for most non-Indigenous people of the era, who may not have been aware of official governmental policies, some of which have finally been acknowledged by the Canadian government to have constituted cultural genocide.

Mary Schäffer, an intrepid explorer who followed the old Indian trails in the first decade of the 20th century, showed a certain perspicacity that was lacking in some of her peers. Writing about her adventures, she reported that she was often asked if she had gone where no person had gone before. Her answer was:

An Indian after all is a "person," and to find a spot where an Indian has not been in that great hunting ground, which has doubtless been hunted over from time immemorial by the plains tribes, would seem an absolute impossibility.

Her response takes on a heart-rending note when she adds:

The caribou, goat and sheep yet wander in these lonely fastnesses, and a few Indians still come to the haunts of their forefathers; but in the further valleys the tepee-poles are fallen and decayed, and thus the story of the passing of the red man is simply and sadly told.[14]

Of course, the "red man" was not gone, but variations on this idea of "the dying or vanished Indian" have long been unpleasant themes perpetuated by non-Indigenous peoples in North American culture. Nevertheless, Christianized but also marginalized[15] Indigenous people do not figure as major players in the adventures which were to enfold in their traditional territories and sacred places after the arrival of the railway. Consequently, the story that follows is primarily one of immigrants and settlers, tourists and visitors.[16]

As the largely unobserved drama in the Indigenous population ensued, the upper-middle-class Victorians had been busy packing trunks destined for "exotic places" all over the Empire and beyond. They were a hardy lot, eager for adventure, who not infrequently travelled with items such as pith helmets, mosquito netting, butterfly nets, jars for collecting, notebooks for sketching and recording almost everything, survey gear, sturdy boots, hunting costumes and of course firearms. It was an era of excited discovery and scientific exploration extending into the Edwardian period. Their travels saw them on safari in Africa, recording (and unfortunately collecting) exotic bird, plant and animal species; hunting tigers in southeast Asia, searching for lost cities in sundry places and trying to gain a greater understanding of the ancient civilizations of Egypt, Mesopotamia and others. There were cohorts in America recording Indigenous languages and exploring cities built by peoples who, from a colonial viewpoint, had appeared to have vanished from the Southwest. These explorers also shared in the far-flung travel and adventure of the Europeans, who were simultaneously exploring their own mountain terrain.

Thomas Cook began tours to Switzerland in 1863.[17] Walking holidays in the Alps eventually became fashionable. But even earlier than this, mountains had been climbed, ushering in a "golden age of mountaineering" in 1854. Following on its heels, climbers began seeking out summits in faraway places. And not just men were alpinists. A surprising number of the disenfranchised weaker sex, greatly hampered by their long skirts and woefully inappropriate footgear, made good on their demand to summit too.

With completion of the transcontinental track, the Canadian Pacific Railway (CPR) began a vigorous advertising campaign:

> The Switzerland of America. Banff. Lake Louise. Lakes in the Clouds. Field. Glacier. These famous resorts for Alpine Climbers are reached only by the incomparable trains of the Canadian Pacific Railway.[18]

A later promotion sought to lure visitors to the mountains with a truly compelling promise: "Keep your youth!" The ad went on to exhort the potential traveller to "come and enjoy great sport where invigorating mountain air revitalizes every tired nerve."[19]

To climbers, adventurers and tourists thirsting for unspoiled horizons – and perhaps revitalization – the Canadian mountains quickly became an alluring and even status-enhancing destination. An elderly dowager – circa 1890 – was overheard by a passerby in a London park to remark to her young aristocratic companion: "Yes, Gerald, you are perfectly right to go to the Rockies; all the best people go to the Rockies nowadays."[20]

Beginning in 1899 the CPR employed Swiss climbing guides in order to keep paying tourists safe and to promote the company's steamships and passenger trains and the luxurious hotels which serviced them. It should be noted, though, that not all of the CPR properties were glamorous at first. As pulling heavy dining cars over the mountains was too challenging for the locomotives of the day, three "restaurant stops" had been built in 1886: Fraser Canyon House, near North Bend; Mount Stephen House, in Field; and Glacier House, near Rogers Pass. A small log structure built at Lake Louise in 1890 burned down in 1893, and was rebuilt the next year in a much more hotel-like incarnation. Gradual additions modernized the hotel. In 1924, however, another fire occurred, which destroyed the older, wooden wing but left the newer, modern wing intact. By 1925 the architecture of the hotel reflected its current "chateau style."

It was in the Canadian wilderness that Edouard Feuz senior, born in 1859 and previously the head mountain guide at Interlaken, Switzerland, found himself in 1899 the first "properly accredited" Swiss guide enticed to Canada by the CPR.[21] He became the lead mountain guide and was stationed at Glacier House, one of the "restaurant stops" in the Selkirk Mountains. Situated right beside the tracks and initially possessing only six hotel rooms, Glacier House quickly became the first centre of alpinism in North America. By 1906 its initial meagre offerings had expanded to include "fifty-four additional rooms, baths, billiard room, bowling alley, central heating and even an elevator."[22]

As the head guide, Feuz engaged the services of additional guides and immediately hired his close friend Christian Häsler to accompany him on his first season in Canada. Charles E. Fay,* a professor of modern languages at Tufts College and a climber who first came to Canada in 1890, said of the two: "No pair of twin brothers were more nearly duplicates in raiment, no two guides ever more supplemented one the other in excellencies."[23]

All the guides Feuz hired signed contracts with the CPR on a season-to-season basis. And because they returned to their homes and families in Switzerland each autumn, they were paid in Swiss francs. Depending on their own aspirations and how well they were perceived to do in their jobs, specific guides may or may not have been offered additional contracts. In addition to hiring, Feuz assigned jobs and was responsible for paying cartage, livery and additional hotel expenses.

The CPR had a few strategic challenges with respect to hiring Swiss guides, not the least of which was communication: Feuz and Häsler spoke absolutely no English. To meet this problem, the CPR enlisted the services of an Englishman, Charles Clarke, who spoke Swiss and French, to accompany the guides and serve as their translator.

With the language barrier somewhat mitigated, the guides were soon leading guests across enormous

* Charles E. Fay (1846–1930), a founder of the Appalachian Mountain Club and the American Alpine Club who made a total of 25 trips to Canada to climb.

glaciers – one of which ran right to the dense old-growth forest of cedar and hemlock behind the hotel – and to the tops of magnificent quartzite peaks. Guests raved about the cozy hotel and the beauty of the Selkirk Mountains. A typical testimony – one amongst many – recorded in the Glacier House Scrapbook in 1899, proclaimed, "My wife & I have travelled for nearly 40 years all over the world & both agreed that the scenery at Glacier House is the finest we have seen in Europe, Asia, Africa or America. We have been most comfortable here & only wish we could stay longer."[24] A visitor to Glacier House in 1907 limited his superlatives to a more narrowly defined geographic region: "This place even surpasses anything I have seen in Switzerland or Tyrol. It is beyond all description."[25]

While his father was away guiding on another continent, the young Edward – although still a *Träger* (a porter or guide in training) – was already earning a reputation for his mountaineering skills at home in the *Berner Oberland*. He was praised for his stamina and adeptness in handling mountaineering challenges, and by the time he was 17 years old there were clear indications that he would develop into an exceptionally good guide.

In 1902 the elder Feuz arrived home after finishing his fourth season in Canada to hear reports of his son's growing proficiency, and announced, "Next year you're coming to Canada with me." There had never been any question of challenging the paternal command. That winter, Edward taught ice skating, and when spring came he left his mother and siblings to accompany his father on the long journey.

Sometimes Edward told this story with an implication that his father had been slightly jealous of his success. On other occasions the story reflected a father's pride in his son's achievements. Edward had great respect and affection for his father, which seems to have been reciprocated, but considering inherent tensions between fathers and sons, and given that Edward senior had ambivalent feelings about being away from home, likely both versions of the story were true.

Reaching western Canada from Switzerland in those days entailed at least two weeks of travel: first to England, next by steamship from Liverpool – across all that water, as Edward put it – and then an additional four days by train from Quebec, through Ontario and continuing west across vast stretches of "bald-headed prairie." On his first trip to Canada, in 1903, Edward quickly grew weary of all the flatness. He was relieved to arrive in Canmore, a coal mining town and division point for the CPR, where, close to the tracks, he was greeted by the peaks of the Three Sisters. Finally they had reached the eastern slopes of the Canadian Rockies.

From Canmore, passengers began what was (until recent history)* one of the most scenic train journeys in the world. Soon they arrived in Banff, with views of that

---

* Regular CPR-run passenger service was discontinued in 1978. Passenger service was transferred to VIA Rail, but the latter discontinued its historic (CPR mainline) passenger service in 1990. The Royal Canadian Pacific (using historical cars) and the Rocky Mountaineer (with modern cars) offer luxury train experiences on the historic mountain portion of the line.

town's signature peaks – Cascade and Rundle – on opposite sides of the tracks. Following the Bow River Valley, they passed Castle Mountain – looking exactly like such a fortress – and headed on to Laggan (the old rail station for Lake Louise) on their way up to Kicking Horse Pass, which crosses the Great Divide and thus was the highest point on their journey. From there they travelled down the Big Hill, which was not at all a misnomer, as by that point they were proceeding along a frighteningly steep gradient of 4.5 per cent,[26] in order to reach the small railway town of Field and Mount Stephen House, one of the CPR restaurant stops.* Farther along the track the train stopped at a small teahouse, giving passengers a chance to see Natural Bridge – the result of work the roiling Kicking Horse River had done to carve its way through solid rock. This point in the track was also close to Emerald Lake and another CPR property, a small chalet, Swiss-like in appearance, which was built in 1902 and was accessed from Field by tally-ho, a horse-drawn carriage.

After descending the rugged Kicking Horse Canyon, the train pulled into Golden. This is where the Kicking Horse River joins the Columbia River in the Rocky Mountain Trench. Here the Rockies end and to the west of the trench the Columbia Mountains (composed of the Purcell, Selkirk, Monashee and Cariboo ranges) begin. Continuing west, once the Purcell trench was crossed, passengers finally arrived in the Selkirks. At Rogers Pass,

* In 1909 the Spiral Tunnels were built, which moderated the grade on this portion of the journey to a more reasonable 2.2 per cent.

from the right side of the tracks, Edward could see Mount Tupper, a peak about which A.O. Wheeler allegedly remarked, "No man in hell can go up that mountain."[27] On the left side of the track he saw Mount Macdonald for the very first time and soon disembarked at his new home, Glacier House.*

Rising gloriously above Glacier House is the dramatic two-thousand-metre pyramid that is Mount Sir Donald. Although Sir Donald had been ascended for the first time in 1890, for most climbers it was (and is) an irresistible beacon. Not surprisingly, taking mountaineers up this peak was a regular occurrence for the guiding community. Edward estimated he had guided this summit ten times in a single summer season. It is a long trek and even today it is not unusual for climbers to underestimate the endurance challenges of Sir Donald, or to find themselves enveloped in a sudden mountain storm.

The usual route to the summit approximated the right-hand skyline (as depicted in A.O. Wheeler's drawing of Uto and Sir Donald).** By 1907 Edward had found a 60-foot chimney (over 18 metres in height) which apparently made the route safer (as it avoided a couloir) but more

* Edward actually spent his first few weeks in the mountains at Field and then Lake Louise, where his father was stationed, but he settled into Glacier fairly quickly. It should be noted that peaks climbed were not necessarily limited to those in the immediate vicinity of hotels. Early guides stationed at Field included Häsler, Fritz Michel and Christian and Hans Kaufman.

** The first ascent, by E. Huber, C. Sulzer and H. Cooper, was by the southwest face and south arête.

difficult. It was composed of three pitches (rope lengths), the upper third of which was hard "owing to the absence of hand-holds & the fact that the walls [of the chimney] are too far apart to be used at once."[28] What the writer meant is that when climbing a chimney feature, one is often able to use holds on both sides of the chimney. If it is narrow and seems holdless one can sometimes "wedge" oneself, back against one side, feet against the other, in order to inch upward using oppositional force.

The now popular steep but pleasantly solid northwest arête of Mount Sir Donald, or the left-hand skyline, was first climbed in 1903 by Feuz senior, who climbed several other routes on the mountain for the first time, and fellow guide Christian Böhren, who two years earlier, along with Christian Häsler, had achieved the first ascent of another impressive pyramidal summit, Mount Assiniboine, with James Outram. To give some perspective on what climbing Mount Sir Donald would have meant for tourists setting off from Glacier House, the first ascent and descent of this route, which occurred in 1919, took the A.H. MacCarthys 15 hours and 12 minutes.[29] And, the time it took them was impressively expedient. Such a lofty goal, meant literally and figuratively, was only suitable for the most fit and intrepid of tourists.

During their first summer in Canada together father and son climbed a variant on Mount Macdonald (the mountain through which the Connaught Tunnel would be built). This was Edward junior's premier first ascent. However, this turned out not to be the very first time the mountain had been climbed, a fact which was known from the presence of a railway spike on the summit, but it likely was a first ascent by the route they travelled, which was up from the tracks.* They climbed numerous other peaks in 1903, and, as he had in Switzerland, Edward was once again making a very positive name for himself, as his *Führer-Buch* (or guide-book) attests.

The *Führer-Buch* contained a guide's proof of certification, a list of regulations and also blank pages so that clients could record their impressions of both their guide and the climb. Anyone considering an outing with a Swiss guide had the right to inspect this record before setting off on a trip with him. In 1903 Edward was still a guide in training. Had he been in Switzerland, he would have carried most of the weight for the party – up to 35 pounds. When the aspirant guide was considered ready, he would participate in a three-week examination. He would be expected to demonstrate mastery of a number of subjects, including weather, qualities of diverse types of terrain (snow, ice and rock), client management, first aid, map reading and languages.[30] With successful completion of the examination the guidebook was updated to document the applicant's new independent "guide status," and he was given an attractive badge to reflect his certification.

Edward passed his examination in 1908, but in an entry in his *Führer-Buch* much earlier than this, dated July 16, 1903, one Raymond Homby remarked of Edward, "The

---

* First ascents are recorded not only in terms of the first person to climb a mountain by any route, but also by climbing to the summit by a new route.

ability he shows for his work is quite outstanding in a person still as young in years."[31] In August that same summer J.M. Cochrane wrote:

> In all my mountain climbing experience I have never been fortunate enough to have had as companion in undertakings difficult and perilous as trustworthy a guide as Mr. Eduard Feuz Jr. One may follow him anywhere in this region and feel perfectly safe. Mr. Feuz certainly knows his business.

When he received this remarkable praise – from a seasoned climber who was not unaware of the inherent dangers in climbing – he was only partway through his first season in Canada and a mere 18 years old. Similarly, J.H. Batcheller, who climbed Mount Sir Donald on September 2, 1903, guided by both Edwards, senior and junior, said of junior that "for so young a lad his ability is very great." He went on to say Edward "displayed the same cool, sure-footed ability which promises so well for his future when he reaches the full rank as guide."

Two years before reaching this "full rank," Edward led Cornelius and Allan Kitchel up Terminal Peak, immediately southwest of Mount Sir Donald. His clients wrote that they had been "halted by a very treacherous bergschrund [a crevasse, or crack which forms on a glacial slope] which we finally crossed in safety thanks to the skills and judgment of Feuz." They reached the summit by climbing the face above the bergschrund. It was the first time Edward had been the sole guide on the first ascent of a mountain. The Kitchels' comment about him read: "Although this was the first ascent, he seemed to know by intuition the best way to go and in coming down displayed excellent judgment, and by taking us along the eastern arête avoided the bergschrund entirely and saved time."[32]

For his part, Edward was smitten with the Canadian mountains and had no greater joy than helping people climb them. Later in life he said, "I was just crazy for this country; that's all there was to it." He was not exactly smitten with Canadian winters, however.

Although all the other guides returned to Switzerland at the end of Edward's first season, he remained behind in order to learn English – and he stayed in Canada for another year after that. During winter at Glacier House he did whatever he could to assist the hotel manager, Julia Young. Even in the winter months two trains per day (one from the west and one from the east) still stopped to allow passengers to have meals, and some guests stayed overnight to take a break from their travels. There was plenty for Edward to do. He helped out in the office and in the kitchen, and it was also his responsibility to meet the trains, welcome guests and make sure the platform was cleared of snow in time for their arrival. He carried guests' baggage to their rooms and handled provisions delivered to the hotel, along with the mail.

Guiding did not continue in winter in Canada; mountain climbing was confined to the summer months. Unlike today there was no "mixed alpine climbing," no ice climbing, no ski guiding. However, it would appear that Edward was enticed to continue his adventures, at least to some extent, during his first winter, because his *Führer-Buch* indicates he climbed a peak on February 4, 1904, with J.C. Herdman, a clergyman from Calgary with a Doctor of Divinity degree who would become a long-term client. The plan initially was to attempt to ascend Mount Abbot on snowshoes. But although they abandoned the snowshoe idea because conditions proved to be too dangerous, they managed to make it to the summit without them. After this ascent Herdman wrote of his young guide that he "acted splendidly throughout: he was surefooted, coolheaded, possessive of good judgment in meeting the unusual conditions of a mid winter trip."

Edward was putting on a brave front. He was desperately lonely in a strange, unfamiliar and cold country with its extraordinarily long winters. Plus, he could not communicate, felt completely isolated, and was again experiencing homesickness. Edward's misery was so intense that when reflecting on it decades later he wondered why he had not developed more symptoms than mere homesickness.

Julia Young, born in 1853, was warmly regarded by all the guests and staff of Glacier House and even had a mountain named after her. Young particularly liked Edward's father, and it distressed her to discover that his son was spending long winter nights walking the railway tracks out of sheer boredom. She decided to take young Edward under her wing, to keep an eye on him and encourage him to really learn English. Two nights a week she sat with him at the fireside and taught him to read. To

Edward she would always be a second mother and he was grateful for the attention she paid him. And, under her tutelage, his English language skills quickly improved.

Edward's need for English lessons had become painfully clear on only his first or second outing onto the "Great Glacier" (the Illecillewaet) the previous summer, when he was asked to take a couple on a roped walk. This short trip required him to chop some steps in the ice, and in those days the spectacular glacier possessed massive towers of ice. As they moved closer to these intimidating-looking towers, the man asked him a question, to which Edward responded, "No." Much to Edward's annoyance, and confusion, they had progressed for only another five to ten minutes when the man asked the question again, to which Edward again responded, "No," and proceeded upward. Finally, the man gave a little tug on the rope, stood his ground, and asked the question for a third time. Edward gave the same response. This time the man pointed down the slope, and Edward, more confused than ever, acceded to their now obvious wish to be taken back to the hotel. Arriving at the hotel in a state of consternation, Edward rushed to a bellboy friend, one of the few people who could understand him a little, and asked what the apparently problematic word in the man's question meant. Mortified when he learned that the man had been asking, "Is it safe?" Edward went out of his way to avoid the couple for the rest of the evening.

In summer, it was easier for Edward to adjust than it was in winter, as he was busy guiding. Also, his father, along with Häsler Sr. and other contracted guides,* had returned from Switzerland and the lodge was filled with guests, some of whom stayed for weeks at a time.

After his first two lonely years, Edward began travelling back to Switzerland for the winters, with the rest of the guides, where he taught figure skating and was a much happier fellow. CPR-employed Swiss guides returning to their hometowns enjoyed a special sort of prestige,[33] and Edward's first ascents in a faraway place made him quite unusual amongst his peers. He also found a love interest in Canada, an Englishwoman, the manager of the curio shop at Mount Stephen House, who was eight or nine years older than he. One year, on the long journey between Canada and Switzerland, he visited his sweetheart in London, where they joined the throngs – purportedly totalling eight million people – drawn to the 1908 Franco-British Exhibition at Shepherd's Bush. She was not to become his wife, though.

In a tongue-in-cheek essay describing her infatuation, Ethel Johns wrote:

> While we were waiting [at the train station] one of my long-cherished dreams came true. I saw a Swiss guide in the flesh. So many of one's dreams are spoiled in the realization; but that guide was, as the

---

* Although there was a fair amount of flux in where guides were stationed, where they climbed and how many seasons they worked, records from Glacier House would indicate that early guides there included Jacob Müller, Christian Böhren, F. Michel and Karl Schullenger. Christian Jorimann was stationed intermittently at Lake Louise.

Virginian puts it, "better than I dreamed." He wore the official badge on his coat lapel. He even sported the Tyrolean feather. His boots were as thick and full of nails as I had hoped. He carried an ice-axe, a rucksack and a coiled rope. I walked round him at a respectful distance and regarded him from every angle. He was a most satisfying person.[34]

There was no more fitting romantic symbol of the early tourist era in the Canadian mountains than the Swiss guide, and this was actively marketed by the CPR to the extent that, according to Edward, not much climbing actually occurred in the early years.

On the long journey from Switzerland by steamship and rail, the guides were scheduled for stops in the major cities – London, Montreal and Toronto – where marketing activities had been planned. Edward was made to walk about the cities not only in his climbing clothes but also carrying his rucksack and gear. He found doing so to be very embarrassing and somewhat akin to announcing the circus had come to town. The guides were asked to stand on ledges atop tall buildings and pose in rock quarries – activities they understandably viewed as demeaning. Photographs taken on such occasions appeared in newspapers and brochures to entice the curious to book a holiday to the Canadian Alps, where the exotic guides could be seen in their natural habitat and perhaps even engaged for an adventure or two.

In another publicity campaign, Edward Whymper, the English "conqueror of the Matterhorn," was brought to

Canada with four Swiss guides in 1901 and made several other trips over a number of years up until 1909. The hope was that he would climb Canada's Matterhorn, Mount Assiniboine, which would have had impressive publicity value for the "Switzerland of America," but he went nowhere near the mountain on his first trip and appeared uninterested when he did actually see Assiniboine.[35] The campaign was generally a failure, and Canadian climbers eager to fawn over the legend were disappointed that he did not write much about his experiences. It seemed that Whymper was unimpressed. To provide some context for that, though, by the time Whymper came to Canada he was old and dissipated, having been traumatized by his Matterhorn experience, which had resulted in the death of four people when the rope broke on the descent of the mountain. Whymper habitually drank to excess, to the point of committing improprieties which were shocking breaches of Edwardian mores, such as walking naked through the halls of Mount Stephen House.

According to Edward, Whymper was regarded with suspicion and frequently distaste by the guides. The first reason for this was that rumours were still circulating in the old country – decades after the event – about what actually happened in 1865 on "the day the rope broke." Secondly, it was often felt his attitudes were supercilious and that he did not treat his guides well. Nevertheless, he was acknowledged by the general (amateur) climbing community to be one of the best climbers of the 1860s and '70s.

The completion of a new hotel at Lake Louise and the

closure of Glacier House, both in 1925, marked a pivotal year in which Canada's alpine centre shifted from the Selkirks to the Rockies. Unlike Glacier House, which was known for its "home-like atmosphere and … informal hospitality,"[36] Chateau Lake Louise gradually morphed into a glamorous destination, an aura it maintained until the Second World War. Travelling to the lake formerly entailed riding in a pony-drawn cart from the train station at Laggan. Later, a tramline up to the lake was constructed, but unfortunately it was removed from operation in 1930. In the modern era, enormous Disneyland-esque parking lots were built at the lake to accommodate motor travel, which included, and continues to include, tour buses disgorging their passengers. At times, in prime summer tourist season, the lakefront can be extremely congested, but it was not always so.

Despite the fact that the facade has always seemed to resemble a prison,[37] the building did take advantage of its stunning location, and in contrast to some of its more rustic antecedents, the Chateau was built to inspire a sense of grandeur. A series of huge, vaulted widows in the lobby – and also in what until recently was the main dining room – framed the long, glaciated and imposing north–south ridge of Mount Victoria, an awe-inspiring view which rightfully has become iconic. The grounds were landscaped in a riot of colour in what became its signature poppy garden. Adjoining the hotel, again with view windows so as to appear contiguous with the lake, was a beautifully designed outdoor swimming pool, built in 1926.

Guests dined in the splendour characteristic of the period, to live music, all coveting the best tables along the windows. Tables were set with real linen and a full complement of silver and glassware. Men were asked to leave the lobby if they were not wearing a jacket, and it goes without saying that dining was formal. Staff were attentive to the smallest detail of guests' needs, while remaining as unobtrusive as possible. There was a separate staff elevator; repairmen were required to don a jacket before emerging on a guest floor. Most of the guest rooms were small by today's standards, as there was a greater emphasis in those days on communal activities. Although one could write or read in one's room, cozy chairs in the lobby beckoned. Writing desks were strategically positioned in front of the picture windows, and even if one were only writing postcards, claiming one of these desks held more than a little inspirational appeal.

After dinner one could relax in the lobby, take a peaceful stroll along the lakeshore or paddle a canoe by moonlight. And of course there was the grand ballroom, with windows looking out to Mount Fairview, where one could dance the night away to the hits of the day. During the day, guests could choose among trails ranging from gentle strolls to rigorous hikes leading to a variety of destinations. A charming, sheltered viewpoint could be found only a short distance along the lake. More ambitious guests ventured to similar shelters higher up, either on the flank of Mount Fairview or atop the Big Beehive, or hiked to small alpine lakes referred to as "the lakes in the clouds." By 1927 they could walk all the way to the

Plain of Six Glaciers for a piece of pie and a cup of tea. If one were lucky, the already dreamlike atmosphere at Lake Louise would be augmented by the sonorous tones of an alpenhorn, played some two kilometres from the hotel by Edward, where the presence of large cliffs at the lake's inlet would produce an echo.

As with Glacier House and Stephen House, the option of hiring a guide at Chateau Lake Louise had always been used to entice the more adventurous traveller to consider a range of off-the-beaten-track adventures in these pristine mountains. Guided glacier walks were available, as were single-day climbs and even multiple-week expeditions, which could and frequently did include first ascents of mountains.

Once mountaineering activities had consolidated at Lake Louise, the guiding staff coalesced into a more or less permanent configuration. For approximately 30 years this consisted of Edward (Eduard) and his brothers, Ernst (Ernest) and Walter, along with Rudolf (Ruedi) Aemmer and Christian Häsler the younger, who was called "Chris" by clients (his Swiss nickname was "Chrigel").

The most obvious difference between Canada and Switzerland to Edward – a fact which would strike anyone at first reflection – is the sheer number of mountains and the huge area they occupy relative to his homeland. Of course, climbing was essentially new in Canada, most peaks had not been climbed, and there was so much wilderness. The appeal of first ascents is obvious. Edward's ambitious approach to mountains, however, was not oriented toward thoughts of records or fame. When asked later in life whether or not he knew he was making history, he responded that he never thought about it, and I think this was true. He was just obsessed.

While wilderness was an exciting idea for tourists, it was a lot more complicated for guides here than in tamer Switzerland. Clients and guides there descended mountains to trails (and trains), spending their nights in huts, hotels and the like. And unlike in Canada, they were unlikely to encounter predators. Thus the mountain guide in Canada needed to develop ancillary skills. Jasper R. Young, a client from Glasgow, Scotland, remarked in 1916: "I soon found out that Edward possessed qualities quite unusual in a Swiss guide, as he proved a good woodsman, camper, cook and packer."[38] It was an accolade of the kind Edward had been drawing for some time. A 1907 first-ascent party on Mount Begbie, near Revelstoke, had previously made numerous unsuccessful attempts on the mountain with "Canadian guides." One of the climbers, Rupert W. Haggen, commented in Edward's guide-book: "His bush work was superior to anything we have seen in the mountains, as he led us always to exactly the point we were aiming at, although it was impossible to see ahead for any distance in the timber."*

In Switzerland, years of climbing had "cleaned" many of the routes, whereas in Canada – especially in the Rockies – loose rock was a constant hazard which confined most ascents to the ridges (where the objective hazard was lessened). Edward described climbing in the

* See Edward's *Führer-Buch*.

Rockies this way: "Before you grab it [a handhold] you test it. Always. And the same with the feet. Don't just jump up on any ledge. You have to test it first."[39]

People today who are familiar with the allure of powder skiing would be puzzled by Edward's opinion on this matter. Snow in Switzerland, he felt, was more amenable to skiing because "it packs better." This was because "in three or four feet of snow [and on the old-style narrow, wooden skis] you sink right down to your knees."[40] Champagne powder was not lusted after in those days, and winter in Canada was harsh, making outdoor sports anything but pleasurable for the Swiss, who enjoyed more salubrious winters at home. Nevertheless, the guides primarily used skis for transportation in winter, in large part replacing the traditional Canadian mode of travel – snowshoes.

Another positive for Switzerland, Edward felt, was the *Kameradschaft* which developed between guide and client, as both would return to a busy hut or hotel for a drink and a meal. For Edward in Canada there was much more isolation, especially after the alpine centre moved from Glacier House to Lake Louise. Glacier House was seen as more of a relaxed and egalitarian environment. The Chateau was much more formal. Edward might have been invited in for a drink, but then the guests would carry on with the remainder of their evening, while the guides were expected to return to their own accommodation, which was separate and a little distance from the hotel. They missed the culture of Switzerland. As recently as the early 2000s an old Swiss guide, Bruno Engler, bemoaned the lack of proper "mountain music" at local ski events – he meant Swiss music.

Despite the various allures of home and of Switzerland, Edward would spend 78 years in the Canadian mountains, and after 1912 he never left North America. He had no interest in pursuing any other vocation. His passion for the climbing life was insatiable. At age 53 he was quoted as saying, "I wish that I weren't going to get old, that I could start all over again, for there are many fine peaks out there that have never been climbed."[41]

Two years later he would climb the highest peak in the Canadian Rockies. Mount Robson, a veritable giant relative to most other summits in the Rockies, soars to 12,972 feet [3954 metres]. It was climbed for the first time in 1913 by the Austrian guide Conrad Kain, with Albert MacCarthy and William Foster.

One might wonder why Edward would wait until his mid-50s to climb such a summit. The first thing to understand is that Edward was not a free agent. He was an employee of the CPR and very much subject to their whims and dictates, that is, if he wished to keep his salary and the security of a job. Mount Robson, on the other hand, is north, near Jasper, in Canadian National Railway (CNR) territory and thus was not a "CPR mountain." Its presence in CNR country meant that Edward was not allowed to climb it, even if, or especially because, it was a high-profile climb. This reasoning sounds odd and makes no sense to us today, but it shows how controlling the CPR was and how competitive the two railway companies were.

Katie Gardiner, an Englishwoman, was 54 years old in 1939 when she approached Edward about climbing Mount Robson. An intrepid climber who had been introduced to the sport as a 10-year-old by her father in Switzerland, Gardiner had spent years as an adult climbing in both Canada and New Zealand. In 1933 she was assumed to have died on Mount Tasman on the South Island of New Zealand. She and her guide spent eight nights in a crevasse on Fox Glacier as a storm raged above them, but they lived to tell the tale of their near starvation.

Undaunted, Gardiner was eager for further adventures. She had made two unsuccessful attempts on Mount Robson, with CN guides, and beseeched Edward, who had never even seen the peak, to get her up the mountain. Agreeing to put forward her case, Edward went to battle for Gardiner and for himself, as it would probably be his only chance to summit this important mountain.

T.E. Chester, the manager of CPR Hotels at the time and thus Edward's boss, was not easily persuaded and flat out forbade Edward to go, as doing so would be, as he put it, "advertisement" for the CNR. Edward seized upon this reasoning. He argued essentially that Gardiner, who was well known, had used CPR transportation services (both trains and steamships) for years, an opening gambit intended to induce some sense of obligation toward a reliable, long-term customer. He then conceded that, yes, their success would be "all over the papers," but it would be a coup for the CPR, not the CNR. After much back and forth, Chester finally consented, as long as it was agreed there was to be no advance advertising of the event. The deal was sealed with a whisky.

Edward enlisted his friend Chris Häsler, who had always wanted to climb Robson, to go with them, as having two guides would maximize their chances of summiting and also make the climb safer.

Then, from beside the hostile CN tracks, Edward and Chris took a long look at the peak with field glasses and plotted a route. The night before their attempt, they stayed at what was the usual camping spot below a ridge with an alarmingly unstable ice wall above it. They spent a most uncomfortable night for additional reasons as well: as soon as it got dark they were beset by leaping packrats and had to endure the rodents' enthusiasms until morning. Although sleep deprived, the three made it to the summit the next day, August 11. According to Edward, they "had no trouble at all." He felt it was a relatively easy climb, but dangerous and with a disappointing view.

The danger was especially evident on their descent, because temperatures were unusually warm, to the point of thawing the snow. Edward was concerned about avalanche hazard. Further, it was already dusk, and because they had to cross a gully beneath the large and unstable ice wall, they decided to spend the night on the mountain. When they eventually reached their bivouac site, it was strewn with huge blocks of ice that had fallen in the night![42]

Having not yet had enough after their grand achievement, they climbed three smaller summits (St. Nicholas Peak and mounts Olive and Collie) on their way back to Lake Louise. Gardiner then travelled to Montreal, en route to England on what had to have been one of the last tourist liners to cross the Atlantic for a very long time: on September 3, 1939, Prime Minister Neville Chamberlain and King George VI had announced that Great Britain was at war with Germany. A letter from Gardiner dated September 29, 1939, on RMS *The Duchess of Richmond* stationery confirmed, "We left Montreal on Sep. 9th but with enforced waits and a different route it has taken us nearly three weeks to get across, but we hope to land tomorrow."[43] In another year the ship would be transporting secret military equipment across the Atlantic to Halifax.

The Chateau Lake Louise closed in 1942 for the duration of the war, but it was still possible, for those in North America, to book climbs with the guides after that time. Tourists during those years often stayed at Temple Lodge, now part of Lake Louise Ski Resort. As the CPR retained the guides only as "caretakers" from 1942 through 1945, the company did not pay for their insurance. Clients wishing to climb were responsible for paying Edward's insurance as well as for the services of packers.

"He breakfasts on chocolate-covered ice cream before starting out on a climb, and although he is courting sixty-five, he is hard as rocks and tough as a pick-axe and he can scale the side of an ice-sheathed crag with the agility of a mountain goat... He is Edward Feuz Jr., the finest guide in the Canadian Rockies, where he holds a record number of first ascents..."[44]

Despite such testimonies to his continued fitness and

competence, Edward was retired in 1949, as he had reached the mandatory age for all CPR employees. He was released with a $100 per month non-indexed pension and a lifetime rail pass. Fortunately he was able to continue his career, for ten years or so, on a private basis.

But even after his second "retirement" he had still not had enough, and as William Putnam put it, Edward continued to go to "high places" in his 70s, 80s and 90s.[45] He celebrated his 80th birthday with an ascent of the tourist route on Mount Temple, a peak over 11,000 feet high. On that occasion, his wife, Martha, wrote to me that her "husband climbed Mount Temple as he had planned, on Aug. 18 '65, in company of two friends; one gent and one lady. He is very happy to have succeeded without any trouble or mishap – I sure hope that he does not dream up any more real high climbs. You know Temple is over 11,600 ft. high."

After this birthday, being blessed with continuing health and extraordinary fitness, Edward continued his mountain life for another 16 years. He did not do this with an agenda of proving that a person in his 80s and 90s could travel with a pack on his back for hours and choose to sleep on the ground and enjoy it. He was not out to prove anything at all, to himself or anyone else.

Today, we do not have as many stereotypical attitudes about how people should behave at particular stages of life as existed in previous generations. And it is not unusual to see older people not only continuing to engage in their sporting passions but doing them well – sometimes better than everyone else. Their achievements, along with science, continue to demonstrate that much of what we thought about physical limitations in older athletes are myths. In Edward's time, resistance to age expectations – and the capacity to resist – was much more unusual than it is today. But Edward was keen to continue being active in the mountains and doing whatever he could to avoid becoming a stereotypical old man. So he just kept going.

CHAPTER 4

HOW WE CAME TO SHARE THE ENCHANTMENT

Although our yearly excursions north from Los Angeles, in the requisite station wagon, had all the hallmarks of an ordinary summer holiday – a stash of camping gear, soggy tomato sandwiches wrapped in waxed paper, two adults in the front seat (doing whatever adults did other than drive and reprimand) and three enthusiastic but whiny and often combative children in the back seat – these trips were more like pilgrimages than anything else.

The destination was always compulsively the same and was spoken of in reverent tones. Utterances of "Yoho," "Lake Louise" and "Rogers Pass" conjured visions of nearly mystic excitement. It was clearly understood in our family that there was only one type of geography that mattered on planet Earth – mountains, specifically Canadian mountains – and that these were inherently superior to all other geographic wonders. Our parents had come to understand this truth in the four years they worked at two of the Canadian Pacific Railway's mountain resorts.

They had become "mountain crazy" before any of us were even born. They had of course made friends with all the guides at Lake Louise, but a special bond was formed with Edward. They could not, however, afford to hire Edward (who was close to retirement but still working when they met), so instead our parents set out to teach themselves how to climb, along with Arthur Oldfield, another CPR employee. They did share their climbing experiences with Edward after the fact, though. He was usually less than impressed with their route-finding and would often exclaim, "Someday I'll come and get you with a basket!" (i.e., a stretcher, or litter, basket), which translated as "Why didn't you come to me and ask about the safest way up that mountain before you attempted it?" Eventually I was born and the three of us moved to Hollywood, and thus began the Stephens' annual trips.

These always started out with long stretches of sweltering monotony. Occasionally there were heat mirages, but these were only mildly interesting for a moment or so. But then trees began to appear and the anticipation of ecstasy grew stronger the farther north we travelled. Eventually, the picture postcards we had collected from previous pilgrimages became three-dimensional. Glimpsing the first real mountains – whose names we knew – conveyed reassurance that all was really as it should be, and we readied ourselves to participate in whatever adventures should come our way.

Our first stop was always at Dave and Phyllis Smyth's gasoline station, just below Lake Louise, at the junction of the 1A highway, for Canadian chocolate bars, which were twice as costly but deemed better than American ones. Choosing one from the Smyths' vast and mind-dazzling assortment was not always easy. Soon, at the wooden boathouse on the shore of the lake, Edward's kind-eyed younger brother Walter would regale us with pleasantries and mountain tales. Then, while our parents paddled, we sat contentedly in a red canvas canoe, each dragging a hand in the cold, glacier-fed, emerald-coloured water in a kind of contest to see who could stand the sensation of pins and needles the longest. Looking up to the towering peaks, which seemed to embrace us, we dreamed and made vows to someday go up there...

And when we got older, we did. Treks through dense coniferous forests were sometimes accompanied by the sounds of tumbling streams, which spoke with a multitude of voices we strained to understand. Higher, above the trees, we walked through uneven, spongy meadows strewn with wildflowers. These had placid streams, which we crossed with measured steps on wooden bridges, making the most satisfying thumping sounds. Then there was boulder hopping, and still higher, thin shale, like walking on crockery, brought guilty pleasure. More-solid rock beckoned us ever upward.

There were wild animals to be seen roaming free and fish to be caught. We had campfires at night and grew drowsy with their warmth. To us, all experiences in the mountains were adventures to be relished, even the painful fretting over which particular pair of handmade moccasins we should buy – from a selection uniformly beautiful – in Banff (which was deemed a good place to visit when it rained) with the allowance we had worked so hard to save all year long. Of course, all the inhabitants of the mountains were of intense interest to us, but above all others – even bears – we looked forward to seeing Edward.

To us Edward was the very embodiment of mountain glamour. What child would not be impressed by a man who told captivating adventure stories and made sounds like a bear to accompany them? We were spellbound by his words. To this day I can see him sitting next to a wood-burning stove as he and the other adults sipped tea from their bone china cups and took turns at storytelling. To us as children, on the one occasion when he visited us in the city, awakening to a rhythmic thudding sound to discover an ever restless Edward seemed as exotic as discovering a mountain goat pacing our floors. He seemed big with his booming voice and forthright manner, but far from being intimidating, he had a fondness for and real understanding of little kids.

When we visited him, we spent nights in dens where he kept his climbing memorabilia – and his hunting trophies – and fought for the privilege of sleeping next to the bear rug. Predictably, once we were in our sleeping bags with the lights out, we imagined all the animals had come to life. What would start with a few growls now and again would turn into shrieks of giddy excitement, as if we almost believed they were alive. Whenever we became especially noisy, adults would appear to tell us to be quiet and go to sleep. While the laughter would continue, though now more restrained, the sheep, the goats, the bear and even the little marmot would all return to their previous mute and inanimate status. The spell had been broken by the intrusion of adults. But alone in the dark with each other, we were beginning to learn the rudiments of storytelling.

We were also learning about climbing and hiking. The first skill Edward had to teach the aspirant mountaineer, young or old, was how to walk. He bemoaned that no one knew how to walk in the mountains – slow and steady, conserving energy – as opposed to "going to beat the band," as they used to say. "The way I climb, I go very slow. The ones that go fast, they hurt themselves. You must take your time." Going too quickly (and usually in spurts with too many breaks) leads to exhaustion, he explained, and on steeper terrain carelessness can be a serious matter.

Once, when we were all quite young, a great herd of people zipped past us on the trail. Edward, sensing this might be troubling to our young egos, turned to us and whispered, "Don't worry, we'll catch up to them." And we did. And then we passed them. Soon there was no sight of them at all! Edward was right.

We followed in his footsteps most of our waking hours, watching carefully how he placed his hands and feet and how he used his ice axe, on the trail and off. Through forests we went, stepping over logs and bashing through shrubbery. High up, above the trees, we watched him chop steps in ice that was too slippery to negotiate and learned how to test the snow for safety. We walked, scrambled and scampered until our legs ached with fatigue.

Days off often meant picnics. A picnic with Edward would have been considered a strain for someone leading a sedentary life. These were never outings of the drive-to-the-park-and-heft-the-goodies-from-the-vehicle-onto-the-nearest-picnic-table variety. Instead, the focus would be on an activity, such as picking wild berries, but there were always "strolls" in some semi-rigorous context or other. A slightly more strenuous category of event, "stretching the legs," was an activity supervised by Edward the morning after real adventures. Coaxed from our cozy beds around eight o'clock, we would be led on a three- to four-hour walking tour around town, gratefully returning for the sustenance, and more importantly the respite, that was lunch. Prior to any hope of lunch our tired nerves could be subjected to such trials as walking through strangers' backyards (murmuring apologies when possible) as the occasional dog ran snarling toward us or, eminently safer, crossing runways at the airport. Edward did not acknowledge minor impediments, such as barbed wire, to achieving his goals, no matter how small.

Ultimately, one of the three children decided that urban motorcycle riding was safer than mountain climbing and declined to willingly participate in any further vertical pursuits. This defining moment occurred for him while standing at the summit of one mountain – albeit accessed by an easy hike on a well-marked trail – and gazing across at another mountain. Smiling broadly, dad said, "That's where we're going tomorrow," gesturing toward a precipitous-looking glacier. The response was firm, immediate and left no room for equivocation. "No, we're not." No amount of pleading, nor even a desperate exhortation which ended with the guilt-inducing "I bought you new boots!" caused Michael to alter his stance in the slightest; his mind was made up.

A second participant suffered a hiatus of enthusiasm after an unfortunate incident caused her to involuntarily leave a small trail – of droplets of her own blood – on a steep trek to a glaciated mountain pass. The sequence of events which caused the injury led to a severe case of paternal hysteria and subsequently dampened the daughter's willingness to pursue risky ventures. On the bright side, and not long after, Cindy again succumbed to mountain fever. I had an intractable case.

Given we now live in a time when there are innumerable guidebooks for hiking, scrambling, alpine climbing, mixed climbing, sport climbing, multi-pitch (rock) climbing, ice climbing and the relatively "new" sport of bouldering[46] (just what it sounds like), it might seem strange that seeking out the vertical was not always an especially popular pastime in North America.

When we were growing up there was only one mountaineering store we were aware of, in all of Los Angeles. Having had a similar experience in western Canada, a friend tells of travelling to the United Kingdom to purchase her mountaineering boots – a long way to go for a pair of shoes. Now, many areas in California are a mecca for sport climbers and bouldering enthusiasts. Indeed, people travel all over the world to climb rock wherever they find it. While climbing now is rather in vogue – there are indoor climbing walls almost everywhere – decades ago, climbing also meant enduring negative judgments from peers for pursuing what was considered a rather odd passion. Apropos of this, when Edward's brother Walter was asked in 1965 about the status of climbing in Canada, he responded, "In these days it's hard to get people to climb out of their cars and walk a few hundred yards, let alone climb a mountain."[47]

The 1950s glorified the stereotypical North American housewife, in her starched apron, who was proud of her shiny kitchen floor. She always knew her place – a sad commentary on post-war North America – and it obviously was not in the outdoors. Although some may look back now and see a safer, more innocent age, for others it was a time of stifling conformity, not to mention one which was overtly sexist, racist and ageist. Thank goodness there have always been rebels amongst us, contesting the boundaries of gender and age, who could be found in havens such as the Alpine Club of Canada or, when one was extremely lucky, crossing the threshold of Edward's house.

CHAPTER 5

FEUZ HAUS

Six small ersatz-chalet-style houses were built on the side of a hill near the small town of Golden, British Columbia – in the Columbia River Valley – so as to be visible from the railway tracks. The CPR had revised their policy of sending the guides home at the end of each climbing season. Instead, they offered them housing, with the stipulation that they must be married. The latter was a mandate Edward never understood. It was one he personally did not have to worry about by this time, but it did present an awkward predicament for at least one of the guides. Nevertheless, in exchange for uprooting their lives (and adhering to the matrimonial requirement) the guides were promised some security – a five-year contract ensuring year-round employment at the rate of five dollars per day.

And so, beginning in 1912, a small colony of Swiss mountaineers and their families lived scattered down the hill in a kind of hierarchy. Each day, the Swiss flag and the Union Jack were raised, to wave in harmony above the highest chalet, per CPR instruction. The CPR called this lonely and impractical little cluster Edelweiss Village, built two monstrous signs denoting this fact and proclaimed the place to be the home of the Swiss Guides. Photos of the village appeared on postcards, in advertising brochures and even on the railway timetable. The train slowed as it approached the sign, giving railway porters and stewards a chance to point out the picturesque scene and furthering the romantic "ad-copy" image of the guides living happily in their quaint, old-country abodes.

These homes were in fact not at all quaint and bore little resemblance to the Swiss chalets promised. Small, poorly built and lacking insulation, they were scorching hot in summer and freezing in winter. The chalets were not a perquisite of the job, either: each family was charged fifteen dollars per month rent.

The CPR had ambitions to expand upon the Swiss mountain theme and urged Edward to find farmers who would move to Canada. The plan was to sell the prospective arrivals ten-acre parcels, even though most of the best bottomland was unavailable. Edward felt farmers on such small and lesser-quality plots would be unable to earn a living (assuming they had the resources to even consider buying land) and concluded that it would be a raw deal for would-be immigrants. Impelled by memories of his brief but miserable foray into farming life, his response to the company was to declare, vehemently, that he and the other residents of Edelweiss Village were *guides*, not farmers. In other words, they were unsuitable agents to promote this agenda. Ultimately, plans to recreate a Swiss farming community withered.

Edward had no idea that it was not the CPR per se that originated the settlement plan, but a very prominent (and meddlesome) British politician named L.S. Amery, whom he would later guide and speak of kindly. Edward's opinion of the man would have been substantially altered – and not for the better – had he known of Amery's involvement. A member of the privileged class, Amery seemed to brag about his advice to the CPR:

> On my way back to Montreal I suggested to Lord Shaughnessy, the President of the Company, that it would be much better in the long run if he took one of the fertile and uninhabited valleys on the line – I mentioned Golden, which in fact he selected – in order to settle a number of guides with their families, saving the expense of a double journey and helping to develop the country.[48]

Leaving aside the colonial prejudice implicit in Amery's advice, not all of the guides wished to immigrate to Canada, even if it meant an end to their employment. Those who did not find the offer appealing included, most notably, the two guides the CPR had originally hired in 1899. The Feuz patriarch, Edward senior, despite his very positive reputation with guests and numerous accomplishments – including first ascents and becoming known as a Mount Sir Donald specialist – did not want to live at Edelweiss, as he longed for the civility of Switzerland. He was over fifty years old when the CPR changed its policy of hiring guides seasonally. It was unimaginable for him to contemplate bringing his wife and other family members to Canada permanently. Declining the offer of settlement, he retired from the CPR and returned to his homeland, but continued to guide until almost his 70th birthday. A few of his clients were people he had met in Canada who after 1910 travelled to Switzerland to climb with him in the Alps. Having helped introduce adventurers in Canada to the ethos of the Swiss guide, the elder Feuz died at his home in Interlaken on June 12, 1944. His passing was noted in *The New York Times*.[49] Edward's mother, Susanna, lived for four more years.

Christian Häsler Sr., an equally qualified Swiss guide with a commendable Selkirk mountain career – who also co-guided the first ascent of Mount Assiniboine – chose to return home to Switzerland for reasons similar to those of his friend Edward Sr. Häsler came back to Canada after his wife died, and lived at Edelweiss, but it did not go well. He came to a tragic end by his own hand in 1924. Offering no hint of the role he played in the history of Canadian mountaineering, his sad tombstone reads only "Native of Switzerland."

Edward's older cousin Gottfried, who guided in Canada for about six seasons, also decided to forgo immigrating and returned home, where he worked mostly at his original career as a carpenter, though he did venture out to guide as well. In 1927 he and his uncle (Edward Sr.) guided Eaton Cromwell, an American who had climbed extensively in Canada, on an ascent of the Mönch, and at the invitation of one of his favourite clients he made at least one trip back to Canada to guide.

Four younger-generation guides (and one aspirant) did settle in Canada more or less permanently. Along with Edward and two of his brothers (Ernst and Walter), their number included Chris Häsler Jr. and Rudolf Aemmer. For Edward, who moved into his father's position as head guide, there had been very little debate, as accepting the terms of the new contract with the CPR meant he could follow his heart's desire – which was to continue to guide in Canada.

Ernst Feuz, born in 1889, was five years younger than Edward. A physically strong man, he was an excellent climber and guide who had come to Canada for the first time in 1909. Rudolf Aemmer, a childhood friend and, as a teenager, a climbing partner of Edward's, was first apprenticed in the art of carving. After becoming a guide, he too came to Canada (the same year as Ernst) but continued to employ his creative talents carving distinctive edelweiss pins and other jewellery in his leisure time. Both he and Ernst were sent to Glacier House their first year, not only to guide but also to begin learning English as Edward had done – with the hotel's one-of-a-kind manager, Mrs. Young. Three years later, both moved into Edelweiss Village.

Walter Feuz was only 18 when he immigrated with his brothers in 1912. Being of such a young age, he was unable to obtain his *Träger*'s licence before leaving Switzerland. But under the tutelage of his older, fully certified brothers, he too became a mountain guide. An amiable fellow, he had a satisfying guiding career before health problems intervened. Thereafter he ran the Lake Louise boathouse.

Christian Häsler the younger, born in 1889, completed the team. Chris (or "Chrigel"), a cheerful fellow with a penchant for practical jokes, was also well liked by guests and was an entertaining correspondent. Before coming to Canada he had refused promotion to a commissioned rank in the Swiss Army, in a mountain infantry brigade, because it would have interfered with his guiding career.

These five guides, along with their families, packed what household goods they could, bade their farewells and began the journey. After weeks of travel, which was made more exhausting by marketing stops for the CPR along the way, they finally arrived at the train station in Golden. There was no one to greet them. There was no way to get up the hill to their new homes. They stood on the platform, some with feelings of sheer despondency, realizing at that moment the enormity of their situation. Namely, that the ease and familiarity of their Swiss lives had been traded for life in a remote place in the strange country of Canada. Martha, Edward's wife, immediately burst into tears.

There actually had been two people eagerly awaiting Edward's arrival, but they were not people who would be helpful with domestic arrangements. One was Howard Palmer,* a lawyer turned businessman, the other a banker turned botanist, E.W.D. Holway, who had leveraged a serious passion for fungi into a career at the University of Minnesota. Both were eager explorers in the northern Selkirks, the latter having discovered climbing on the

* Howard Palmer (1883–1944) was a Harvard-educated lawyer who never practised law but instead joined his family's Connecticut bedding company. He did extensive exploration and mapping of the Purcell range and wrote the classic *Mountaineering and Exploration in the Selkirks* (see note 50).

cusp of his 50th birthday. They were determined to make a sixth attempt on the highest peak in the Selkirks, the impressive, glaciated Mount Sir Sandford.

Arriving in Golden on June 10, the climbing partners found, instead of Edward, a wildfire threatening to destroy the town. All that the CPR knew about Edward's whereabouts was that there was a Swiss contingent on the train somewhere between Montreal and Golden. The group arrived five days later. Palmer and Holway, mindful of changeable weather, were champing at the bit, but there were barriers to leaving immediately. The immigrants, who barely had time to catch their breath, had arrived to houses which were not yet furnished, the guides' climbing clothes were packed away in trunks, and a Swiss wedding was scheduled for the evening of June 17. Despite whatever celebratory repercussions there might have been, a group of six managed to catch the train the morning after, and thus began the long journey to Sir Sandford.

Edward and Rudolf, carrying their heavy climbing gear, left the train at Donald along with one of the packers and began walking more than 54 kilometres (34 miles) up the Columbia River, in 29°C heat (84°F), to their first camp at the mouth of the Gold River, where they arrived the following day around noon. There they met the other members of the expedition, who had travelled by canoe with most of the supplies. The group succeeded in making the first ascent not only of the elusive Mount Sir Sandford but also of another remote peak, Mount Adamant, before marching out through the forest again.[50]

Adjusting to life at Edelweiss was especially difficult for the women. Martha Heimann was a year older than Edward and had grown up in Grindelwald. She had worked for a dressmaker who had been a neighbour of Edward's family. He used to see the rosy-cheeked girl walking to her special place, atop a cliff, where she liked to spend Sundays reading. Eventually the two went to a dance together and enjoyed each other's company. By the time Edward was convinced to go to Canada for the first time (in 1903), Martha was working as a nanny for a French-speaking family. She was fluent in French, and having grown up in a town where a large number of English people lived, she spoke a fair of amount of English as well, which would later prove particularly useful.

While in Canada Edward found an English sweetheart. But later, on a trip back to Switzerland, he discovered that Martha was "keeping company" with the postmaster's boy. Edward had to admit, the postmaster's boy was very nice. Nonetheless, he felt sad at hearing the news. Sundry questions entered his mind: Had he, even subconsciously, expected Martha to be waiting? Did he really want to marry a young woman who was not Swiss? Reflecting on the matter, he realized that he had liked Martha quite a lot and it seemed he had missed his chance to win her. Eventually it did work out in his favour. Martha, studious by nature, had ambitions to become a language teacher, which was not surprising given her facility with languages. Instead, she married the handsome Edward in 1909.* Their first

* They were married on November 16, 1909, at Grindelwald.

child, Martha Gertrude (called Gertie), was born in 1910, and less than two years later Martha's expectations for the future were dramatically altered when her husband's employment required her to leave her homeland. Their second child, Hedye Elise, who came along in 1912, was born in Golden and completed their family.

Johanna Heimann, 20 years old in 1912, came to Canada with her married sister, Martha, as did the middle sister, Clara, who, like Johanna, was unmarried. The sisters chose to immigrate with Martha, because their parents – Johann, a respected notary (as well as an enthusiastic marksman and singer), and Marianna Inäbit, a midwife – had died and the sisters did not want to remain in Grindelwald on their own.

After immigrating, Johanna worked as a chambermaid, first at Glacier and then at Sicamous. She married Walter Feuz in 1914, and together they had a large family at Edelweiss. The first three children, Doris, Anne and Sydney (Syd), were considerably older than the five that followed: Betty, Paul, Ron (Ronnie), Jean and Lucy – somewhat as if Johanna and Walter had raised two families.

Elise Schmid, born at Interlaken in 1889, married Ernst, who was born the same year* and together they had three children, Frederick (Fred), Alice and Ernest (Ernie). Elise was a strong woman both physically and mentally, but she felt like an outsider and did not get along with the Heimann sisters, who had a very close

* Elise lived to be 100; Ernst died in 1966.

relationship. The situation was not an easy one for Elise.[51]

Clara* and Rudolf Aemmer had two children, Ruedi Jr. and Irwin. Both died as young adults in 1936, so when Rudolf retired, he and Clara returned to Switzerland. Rudolf died in 1973 at his home in Interlaken. Eventually his and Clara's ashes were brought back to Canada so they could be buried with their sons.

Rosa, a Feuz cousin, married Christian Häsler Jr., in Golden's first Swiss wedding. They had two sons together, Walter and William (Billy), but sadly their family would be plagued by misfortune. Not only did Chris's father die under tragic circumstances but Billy's death in 1937 as a result of a freak accident permanently traumatized Rosa. Two years later Chris and the well-known CPR photographer Nicholas Morant surprised a grizzly bear with her cub near Sherbrooke Lake and were seriously mauled. Morant, who had acted heroically, fully recovered from the attack, while Chris died in 1940, not long after fulfilling an ardent climbing ambition, the ascent of Mount Robson. He was only 51. Walter survived his parents and brother but died at 47.

At any rate, when the five young families first found themselves in Golden it was quite an isolated place and little more than a logging town. Their housing arrangement was difficult, as Edelweiss Village, high up on the side of a hill, was a significant distance away from the

---

* This was not Clara Heimann; she married Peter Gattiker and moved to Seattle. To make matters even more confusing, Edward also had a sister named Clara.

actual town. Martha did not like the circumstances such isolation imposed, especially as she already had a young child in 1912 and a second was soon to follow. There was no transportation up the hill, and the village road was too difficult to manage when pushing a pram. She had no choice but to carry the children and leave the pram down below, just one example of the many challenges the other wives would also face. An added difficulty was that the road to their houses was not cleared of snow in winter. The railway line, of course, was cleared.

Once off the hill, there were no roads at all, and since they had no horses, walking the tracks was the only way to get into town, in any season. Despite her parents' protestations, seven-year-old Gertie had insisted on going to school on an especially snowy day. She was walking along, in what must have been very poor visibility, when she encountered a snowplow clearing the tracks and was forced into a deep snow drift. Fortunately she was not seriously injured, but the accident terrified her parents and was a reminder of some of the unusual challenges inherent in their Canadian lives.

While the Heimann sisters had grown up in a mountain village, it was nothing like their new mountain life. Grindelwald was already becoming an alpine destination in the early 1800s, with two hotels steadily attracting tourists, walkers and, within a few decades, climbers. In winter, skating was the preferred pastime; skiing did not come until later. In 1890, when the train arrived, Grindelwald boomed. By 1900 there were eighteen hotels and sixteen skating rinks in town.[52]

Given the sisters' Swiss upbringing, it should come as no surprise that western Canadian life seemed very primitive to them and indeed to all the wives. They had no ambition to become pioneers, but that is exactly what they were now. Daily tasks were huge challenges and there was a dearth of social support and activity. Even though Martha had her sister for company, Edward was gone for long stretches of time. Indeed, he had left (with Rudolf) on a long trip before the families had even fully moved into their new homes. Although he was away from home working to support the family, it was also true that he was leading an exciting and socially stimulating life without Martha. The absence of husbands for extended periods of time was endured by all the guides' wives, and it imposed on them an added burden of responsibility, especially as they were living in such a remote place. It was tremendously challenging for the women, all of whom were new to Canada and most of whom did not speak English.

They also found the climate difficult. Canadian winters in the first half of the 20th century were severe, with much more snow than typically occurs now, and a significantly greater amount than fell in Switzerland. Edward recalled that it was not uncommon to have nine feet of solid snow (not drifts) beside the hotel at Glacier.[53] Winter was also long. And no new shoots burst forth on the immigrants' first spring day in 1913: the temperature in Golden plunged to a record −20°C.

In addition to the diverse adjustments the families underwent, the first few winters were unpleasant for other reasons. After abandoning them at the rail station, the

CPR magnified what seemed like a symbolic gesture by failing to deliver on its promise of a year-round salary. The guides filled in, working at odd jobs such as repairing fences and stacking lumber, but they had no steady way of earning money. When Edward was still returning to Switzerland each winter, he not only made good money teaching figure skating, it was a job with prestige.

In Golden he and the others "practically starved." Desperate, Martha and Edward wrote a letter to the CPR management describing their plight. They received no reply. After several other unsuccessful attempts, they resorted to writing the Swiss consul general in Montreal for help. The employment contract they had signed with the CPR had been broken, they pointed out, and since the result was that they were not able to earn a living in Canada, they simply wanted to return home to Switzerland. Although the CPR never officially acknowledged awareness of any of the letters, Edward's plea to the consul general seemed to have gotten the company's attention, as the guides finally began receiving the year-round salary they had been promised.

Conceding they had a hard and frugal life, the late Jean Feuz Vaughan, Edward's niece (born in 1932), was nevertheless angered by written accounts which suggested that the guides' wives were unhappy. To her, "hard and frugal" did not equate to misery. Furthermore, as a child, she would not have been sensitive to her cousin Alice's perspective, and unhappiness did not reflect Jean's experiences of Edelweiss family life. She described her mother and aunt as having had a congenial relationship, and there was always laughter in Jean's childhood home. She had no memory of ever being punished, nor of either parent finding it necessary to raise their voice. Her father, Walter, an even-tempered, friendly fellow, was shy and reserved. Her mother, Johanna, had a similar personality. She remembered her uncle Ernst as being very likeable, and although possessing a happy demeanour, he too was quiet. In contrast, her gregarious and outgoing Uncle Ed "gloried in talking to people." The family called him "the boss." Still, the brothers, who spent most of their lives working and living together, got along well. Jean never heard any of them argue. Although the standards for how adults were expected to behave around children in those days were different from present norms, this still seems extraordinary.[54]

With no butcher shop down the block, the guides hunted and smoked their own meat. Edward procured fish through dubious means, finding the act of fishing to be a dreary pastime without any inherent interest. One might muse that his disinterest in angling could have been shaped by one that got away, back in 1921. Edward and a client, Henry Hall, were fishing from the shore of a lake when Hall pointed out a big one lurking in the shallows. Edward managed to lure it from its peaceful repose, and when it took the bait he hoisted it high in the air with his makeshift tackle. But the fish managed to free itself and landed with a great *plop* some distance from the water. Edward stared in disbelief as the fish, wriggling mightily, managed to fling itself back into the lake. Thus dinner, having demonstrated its unwillingness to co-operate with that agenda, swam away.[55]

There were frequent meals of deer or goat sausage. When fresh meat was prepared, gravy was made from the jelly. The families grew their own vegetables. Potatoes and other root veggies could be stored in a "cold room" (or root cellar) for the duration of the winter. Other vegetables, including pickles, would be preserved in jars. Martha grew green beans and hung them to dry. There was an abundance of huckleberries to be found in the nearby hills. One of Jean's early fond memories of her dad was the time he returned home with a big grin on his face and carrying a huge pack board laden with sacks of berries he had picked. Johanna made jam from the wild huckleberries and jelly from red currants she grew.

All the cooking in the early days was done on wood-burning stoves and in fireplaces – from roasts and gravies to breads, pies and cookies. Martha got up each morning at five to light the stove, not just for cooking but also to warm the children's clothes before they got out of bed. For most of us today, with our microwave ovens and convenience foods, cooking on a wood stove – and cutting all the necessary fuel before the onset of winter – would seem an inconceivable amount of work, not to mention an impossible expenditure of time. At least it was easier to collect wood in Canada than it had been in Switzerland. Wood being plentiful here, there was no need to dangle oneself over a cliff.

While there was no comprehensive plumbing, in other words, no lavatory, the guides did install the first domestic water system in town by pumping water from a spring into cisterns in their basements. Nevertheless, from washing dishes to sweeping and scrubbing floors, sinks and tubs, ordinary housework was not easy. Washing clothes entailed negotiating a hand-operated wringer. In winter, laundry was hung on a wooden rack in the kitchen to dry, and in warmer weather, on outdoor clotheslines. Then came the ironing. Heavy irons were heated on the stove and then used to press clothing. As if washing, drying and ironing were not labour enough, many of their clothes were handmade. The wives were frugal and did not waste anything. Empty flour sacks were turned into embroidered tea towels and tablecloths. All of the Swiss women belonged to the United Church of Canada Ladies Aid Society. Although they did not necessarily go to church, they baked for the society. Most evenings were spent knitting and mending socks, by the light of coal-oil lamps. Simple holes in socks would be darned, but when the foot part of the garment simply wore out, they would cut it off, knit a new one and attach it to the old legging.

Just getting through the day a century ago was a much bigger chore than it is now, and yet somehow this generation found time for relaxation. They played Jass, a complicated Swiss card game,* or just sat and chatted over tea poured from a china pot into cups with saucers, the latter always resting on an embroidered tablecloth.

* Played with Swiss cards, which are different from French ones. Swiss cards have suits of *Schellen* (bells), *Schilten* (shields), *Eicheln* (acorns) and *Rosen* (roses).

There were a few more-active recreations, some more adventurous than others. Edward, bemoaning that there was not much to do in the early days, used to "ski with the Swedes" because they were the only group of people who engaged in this sport, and the Swiss had brought skis with them when they immigrated. The Swedes also had two horses for skijoring, which consists of harnessing a horse, putting on one's skis and – going! Terrifying though the sport may sound to someone who is not an adrenalin junkie, Edward found it amusing to skijor right into town on an occasional Sunday, in order to "liven things up." Residual tendencies of the *Lausbub* were well-entrenched in Edward's character.

The children entertained themselves mostly at home, if for no other reason than that they were too far from town to do anything there. For winter, though, they had a ski hill, the first one in town, which even boasted a jump. Ice skating opportunities were found by simply walking downhill to the nearest beaver pond. For further entertainment, when they were a little older, Edward bought Gertie and Hedye a piano. The sisters were always perceived by their cousin Alice to have more sedentary interests than herself. Fond of being outdoors, she spent most of her time playing with her brothers. A favourite sport was careening down the alarmingly steep village road on the "caboose," a sleigh her father had made for her.

Edward and his family moved down the hill from their residence in Edelweiss Village to a two-and-a-half-acre property he persuaded the CPR to sell him in 1915.

Monthly payments were deducted from his paycheque; he was certainly not capable of buying the place outright. The setting was idyllic and quiet. On the acreage was a burbling creek and a house with a root cellar. Across a footbridge, Edward had built a charming cabin which was filled with climbing equipment, memorabilia and hunting trophies. Three decades after Edward and Martha moved into their new house, my father wired it for electricity, making it the first residence in Golden with such an amenity. Martha was ecstatic. Imagine flipping a switch and having light and power – a simple cause and effect relationship many of us in the industrialized world take for granted.

After the move, Martha and Johanna continued to spend considerable time together. In later years Johanna drove (her sister did not) and thus had more mobility, but they were able to walk the hill to see each other, and young Jean was able to skate all the way to her aunt Martha's house from her usual skating pond at the bottom of the hill.

Jean, with a slightly mischievous smile on her face, which demonstrated her Feuz heritage, quipped that her uncle Ed was always amiable and lots of fun. She and her siblings were always happy when he and Aunt Martha came to visit. But the most special and exciting visit of the year came on Christmas Eve, the time when Europeans have their major Christmas celebrations. Prior to the festive event, Johanna prepared braided Swiss bread (*Zopf*), called *Züpfe*. Busy for some time before the event, she and Martha baked Swiss treats such as *Shenkli* and *Chüechli*, as well the British-inspired Christmas cake.

When the guests arrived, the *Züpfe* was accompanied by cheese, pickles and glasses of wine. Then, in the most eagerly awaited moment of the children's year, the Christmas tree would be set all aglow with real candles. Tea, coffee and sweets were served, and in this warm and enchanting environment the presents were opened. Jean's eldest brother, Syd, did not remember the ambience of this special night so much as the fact that each house in the village hosted its own party during the festive season. Five times as much celebrating. Five times as much food.

From 1927 and continuing through 1938, Martha spent her summers running a Swiss-style tea house Edward had persuaded the CPR to build above Lake Louise at the Plain of Six Glaciers. Edward originally wanted to build the place as a residence for himself, but the company would not let him. Nevertheless, the CPR agreed to support a teahouse, and the project was to be supervised by Basil Gardom, a company construction foreman who was quite excited by the idea.

The attractive stone and timber structure, still in use today, has a large wraparound balcony on the second floor where guests can relax and savour a view along with their tea and pie. Edward installed the water system for the building and made all of the wooden tables by hand. At the teahouse, Martha performed many of the same tasks she did at home, albeit in a spectacular alpine environment. Plus, she was close to Edward and had her own opportunities to meet the many interesting guests who frequented the mountains in those days. Many times, Edward would bring clients to spend the night at the teahouse prior to their climbs. Martha, with Gertie and Hedye, prepared dinner and breakfast for the visitors so they would be well fortified before starting off on their mountain quests. The sisters, in their traditional Swiss dresses, made a memorable impression on the guests. Late in her life, Gertie reminisced wistfully that the days spent at the Plain of Six Glaciers were amongst the very happiest memories of her life, and she hoped she might see the teahouse again. Hedye, who was less gregarious than her sister, was not as enthused about spending her summers in alpine isolation, no matter how splendid, but doing so could have unexpected benefits.

Tourists have traditionally held some bizarre ideas about wildlife in the parks, so it is difficult to know if this request by one teahouse visitor was tongue-in-cheek or not:

"I'll give you a dollar if you show me a mountain goat," the man said to one of the girls.

"Follow me, mister," was the probably unexpected response.

To the back of the teahouse they went.

"There!" the girl said, pointing to a fine white specimen standing grandly up on the cliff. Smiling, she collected her reward.

The Feuz cousins Syd and Fred (sons of Walter and Ernst respectively) also spent time at the teahouse and were put to work at a young age. Twelve-year-old Syd carried in food supplies in his rucksack, such as eggs, which were deemed too fragile to be packed in by horse. He and Fred were also responsible for chopping wood and bringing it to the teahouse. As each sturdy krummholtz tree had to be cut right down to the ground, it was hard work for the young lads.

Edward's primary summer residence at Lake Louise was Guide House, a log structure built in 1920 adjacent to the lake and still extant, where he and the other guides could be close to the guests for an early morning start or a last-minute day trip. The two-storey cabin had a large fireplace and a wood-burning stove. There was a cozy front room and a dining area in the kitchen. Because he did not like cooking – although he did cook for guests in the backcountry – Edward assigned Walter, the youngest, to be the chef. Unlike his elder brother, Walter learned to produce a very passable apple pie, an admirable skill and one I am sure Edward wished, later in life, that he had acquired. Each evening, by the light of Coleman lanterns, the residents sipped their ritual rum toddies before climbing the wooden staircase and tucking into their beds.

Although Guide House was usually a fairly peaceful place – after all, its inhabitants were used to rising very early most mornings – one dark night was an exception. A tremendous *BANG* at three in the morning startled all the residents from their slumbers. They scurried out of their rooms to see a pair of bare lower legs descending the ladder from the attic. Then the nightshirt came into view and finally the stocking cap. The figure so attired was gripping a rifle in his right hand, which appeared to have a flashlight tied to its barrel. Glowering, he marched past the stunned and staring witnesses into his bedroom and shut the door. Apparently, Ernst's sleep had been troubled by a packrat's nocturnal ramblings. Sadly for the packrat, it was its last ramble.[56]

On occasion, the guides' family members were able to visit. Syd Feuz reminisced that the children were free to stay with their fathers at Guide House whenever they wanted in winter. Ernie, Fred and Syd, all skiers, were allowed to venture across the well-frozen lake and onto the glacier, but within certain boundaries. No skiing into the Death Trap,* a sensible prohibition. Syd's memory was that the adults were always exceptionally kind and tolerant. At least one adult was always available and willing to take them out. They lived an outdoor life most children could only dream about. Although a few of the Feuz boys wanted to become guides, their fathers discouraged them from doing so because of the low wages. Later in life Syd did carry on the Feuz guiding tradition, becoming a ski guide, and enjoyed a 28-year second career. But he'd acquired his basic ski skills way back in childhood, in the early days of Edelweiss Village, when the children had their own ski hill. Syd's skills were also honed on Victoria Glacier.

One day, in no particular context other than the fact that Cindy and I were sitting with him on the steps of Guide House, Edward suddenly proclaimed that he had taken Sherlock Holmes for a walk. Unfortunately, he

---

* The narrow, steep and dangerous route to Abbot Pass.

could not remember which one: William Gillette? Basil Rathbone? Having taken *any* Sherlock Holmes for a walk was an intriguing revelation and brought to mind questions Edward could not answer. Did they share pipe tobacco? Surely they didn't trade hats. Edward would not have coveted a deerstalker, even if it had been Holmes's very own. But however that day went, one can only hope Edward kept "Sherlock" well away from rushing water, so as not to remind him of his Reichenbach Falls trauma.

Some aspects of the work were not as glamorous as taking famous actors on outings. The guides were basically labourers and caretakers during the off-season. On winter days, they would ski in to each of the CPR's "camps" to shovel snow off roofs to prevent them from collapsing under the accumulated weight. They modified sets of crampons specifically for this task so they could stand on the icy roofs without sliding off. Early in the century a camp had been built at Emerald Lake, and there were tents and a tea house at Moraine Lake. In the 1920s Edward and Basil Gardom began scouting locations for additional camps, such as in Yoho Valley and at Lake O'Hara, where a lodge was built in 1926.

Although Lake O'Hara is a beautiful place, Edward grew restless and bored there on long winter nights when he and Rudolf were caretaking. Rudolf began coping with the tedium by carving fancy paper-knives (letter openers) and swallows. Edward did not think he was capable of anything as artistic as Rudolf, but he did believe he might make a few things out of wood and began producing pipe racks and other small objects.

Not even the Chateau was open all year round. This, Edward never understood. Why did the CPR not advertise to tourists who liked to ski and enjoyed other winter sports, as resorts in Europe had been doing since the 1800s? Finally, yielding to Edward's persistent urging, a grand winter opening was held – with plans for ice skating, sleigh rides, curling and tobogganing[57] – but not until 25 years after he retired. Still, a delighted Edward, along with his brother Walter, rode with the hotel manager to the front of the Chateau in a horse-drawn sleigh, officially opening the doors on a sunny and appropriately snowy winter day. The experiment did not succeed in its first year, however, and it would be many years before the Chateau would try again. Today it would be unthinkable to close the hotel for the winter season. But until that day happened, late spring was when a small group, including the guides, would ready the Chateau for opening.

One of the guides' tasks, along with the construction crew, was to fill the ice house, not only with ice but also with sawdust to help insulate it all summer long. Ice from the lake would be sawed into large blocks and hauled off by horses.

Inside the Chateau, everything had to be cleaned and readied for guests. During the 1940s this was a task entrusted to Pat (my mother) and the head housekeeper, both of whom began work several weeks before the rest of the hotel staff arrived. Other workers, such as Mike (my dad), raised collapsed electrical poles and restrung wire that had succumbed to heavy snows. As the Chateau had been built on a swamp, its elevator shafts would fill with water during the winter, and needed to be drained. At times, there was three or four feet of ice in the shafts. Alarming-looking cracks would sometimes appear in the upper storeys of the building, purportedly big enough to put one's fist in, and pipes might have burst.

Repaired pipes still needed water, of course, so Ernst asked Mike if he wanted to accompany him on a short trip to check on the hotel's source of supply. Mike eagerly accepted, not wanting to miss an opportunity for an outing. After strapping on their wooden skis, fitted with skins for traction, the two began slowly making their way uphill toward Mirror Lake, not quite three kilometres away and nestled beneath a rock formation called the Beehive. Mike, tramping along behind Ernst, was becoming impatient with the slow pace. With the special arrogance of youth, he found himself wondering whether the "old man" (Ernst was probably close to 60) would actually make it to his destination. When eventually they did arrive at the lake, Ernst knelt down and put his ear to the wooden pipe. Satisfied he could hear water running, he removed the skins from his skis and without uttering a word simply shot into the dense woods. Mike, an athletic young man, struggled in vain to keep up. Careening down the hill, he found himself perilously close to tree after tree. To avoid slamming into these, he made one anxious jump-turn after another, seemingly in endless succession, hoping his quick calculations for avoiding a collision were correct. Finally arriving at the bottom of the hill, somehow miraculously intact but shaking and drenched in perspiration from his effort, he found Ernst standing calmly with his skis already removed, waiting for him. A duly humbled Mike revised his assumptions about old men, at least fit, tough old men.

On September 11, 1949, sixty people crowded into Guide House for a farewell party in honour of Edward and Rudolf. Both were retiring from the CPR. For Rudolf it really was farewell. Soon he and Clara would be packing their belongings. After 37 years in Canada, they were returning to Switzerland.

The festivities, which featured music, entertainment and a luncheon, were hosted by Margaret Hays, manager of the Lake Agnes teahouse. Norah Campbell, the co-host, read out the congratulatory telegrams and letters. Among messages Edward received was one from the assistant general manager of Western Hotels, who wrote: "Chateau Lake Louise will not seem the same without Edward's smiling and cheerful countenance." And from Georgia Engelhard, at the Chalet Ultima in Zermatt, a letter read: "To my good friend Edward – not only my friend but a truly *great* guide with whom I have had some wonderful climbs beginning in 1927... Thank you, Edward, for those first ascents in the Murchisons...,"[58] she added, referring to two towers she and Tony Cromwell climbed with him in the summer of 1941.

Each honouree was presented with a silver tray. When the celebrations had come to an end, they all linked arms and sang "Auld Lang Syne." It was the end of a long chapter in Rudolf's and Edward's lives and the beginning of a new one.

Long after this event, in 1960, Edward and Martha moved downtown from their acreage to a lot next to their daughter Gertie's house (and also close to their younger daughter, Hedye), where Edward lived for the next 21 years of his life. It was in this house that we spent the most time with the Feuz family.

The house was a modest bungalow, painted pink and white like a fancy layer cake, with a variegated tin roof and dwarfed by a prodigious conifer in a far corner of the front yard. From the front gate in the cotoneaster hedge a straight concrete path lined with flowers led to the front door, though everyone always entered by the side door, into the kitchen. The garage, adjacent to the house, mirrored its design and colour, so that the two were a matched set. The front yard was brilliant with flowers. At the corner of the house a wooden sign read "Ed Feuz." An especially profuse stand of pink cosmos could be seen as one entered the backyard. In the shade of another large conifer was a garden table and chairs. Martha liked to have some California poppies and there was also a large kitchen garden where vegetables that actually tasted like something came out of the earth instead of from plastic packages or cans.

Arriving at Martha and Edward's home with excited anticipation, we were greeted with enthusiastic handshakes and smiles. Sometimes, even before the formalities, Mike would be met by a sheepish-looking Edward holding up for inspection the frayed remains of a power cord. The luxuriously long grass in the front yard was usually a clue that he had once again run over the power cord with the mower. It always seemed to me a pity to cut the grass, and maybe Edward actually felt so too and purposely kept it thick and beautiful. Other than this one unavoidable lapse, Martha and Edward's house and garden exemplified the values of the house-proud Swiss. In other words, everything was neat, clean and orderly, from the tools in the shed to the clichéd "kitchen floor so clean you could eat from it." Floors did not get this way easily. Even in old age Martha scrubbed theirs on her hands and knees. We were so intimidated by the brilliance of the kitchen floor that we quickly whipped off our shoes before entering the house, despite predictable protestations from Martha. "No, your feet will get cold," she would say. "It's no trouble, and we're wearing thick socks," we would reply. Then we would pad toward the most fascinating feature of the kitchen – the sink – and politely ask for a glass of water. It must have seemed a little strange to Martha, who always offered us a cold drink from the fridge, that we preferred water from the tap. But to us, the town of Golden's water supply was of a "designer" type – cold, clean, pure, non-chlorinated – and in stark contrast to the foul-tasting, tepid Angeleno stuff we were accustomed to. Edward and Martha did not know how lucky they were to have such a luxury. They took it for granted. Now gone are the days when we could enjoy pure, untreated water coming out of taps and even drink from most fast-flowing streams without fear of getting sick.

The rest of the kitchen was fairly standard for its time, when such rooms were plain and predictable. There were the usual appliances, a steel and pale-yellow

Formica-topped table and four chairs. Across the kitchen, near the back door, was a utility room, with hooks for jackets and mats for shoes, also neat. On the adjacent kitchen wall hung a barometer and an old wooden clock, a wedding present, which Edward would wind up with a key each night. The next room had a dining table and china cabinet, and adjoining this was the living room with a sofa and chairs and a television. There were doilies on the furniture. Embroidered tablecloths were brought out for tea.

Despite the cheery, welcoming nature of the house and garden, the beacon for us was below, in the basement. The musty but not unpleasant scent of this cave-like place still lingers in my memory. Down there was Edward's workshop, where he spent much time during chilly winters at his hobby of making tables and lamps from burled wood. He made lamps of all sizes from diamond willow, which needed to be cut green, peeled, sanded and then varnished as soon as possible to preserve the natural colour of the wood. Also in the basement were a "cold room" – for storing vegetables and jars of pre-serves – some old trunks, a sink and a washing machine with a wringer. Their beautiful wood-burning stove, its chrome still shining, had been banished to the bottom of the stairs. But in addition to all this was a room separate and apart.

The first thing one noticed when walking into this room – in fact, the only thing one noticed – was that practically every inch of wall space was filled with framed photographs, large and small, mostly black and white but also some colour. There were photos of people and lots and lots of alluring mountains. Each was a story of Canadian mountaineering waiting to be told. Many of these were sent to Edward by friends and clients; many others he took himself. His own photographs frequently accompanied journal articles detailing first ascents and other notable climbs. To Georgia Engelhard, a climber, artist and professional photographer, Edward was not only the best guide in the Canadian Rockies, he was also "the best amateur photographer of that region I know." As the author of an article featuring a selection of his work, Engelhard goes on to say, "He has a true photographic eye as far as mountains are concerned. As I have been enlarging his negatives, I have been amazed how few of them need cropping. Each is beautifully composed. He has the uncanny faculty of seeing true without having to think twice about it."[59]

Viewing these images was an eagerly anticipated ritual. We scanned the walls each year looking for our favourites, absorbing each detail until our imaginations were satisfied. Edward would tell us a story we had not heard, or maybe one we had heard, and would answer questions we might have had, which were usually mundane: How hard is that? Can I go there? Classically beautiful peaks, like the stately Mount Sir Donald, were of special interest to us. Edward made dozens of ascents of Sir Donald when he was stationed at Glacier House. When talking to us about this climb, he said, "You'll get to the first pitch [the beginning of actual climbing] and you'll wonder 'how the hell will I get up there?'" In regard to other mountains he would remark, "This part will make you smile" – an understated way of saying "you'll be more than a little nervous."

Amongst all the images squeezed into this room, one of my childhood favourites, and no doubt the favourite of many children, was a black and white photograph of "Janet," taken by Edward. The scene is Lake Louise in winter, Mount Victoria in the background, with snow deep on the ground and adorning the trees. Janet, looking decidedly wolfish, is standing with her attention directed toward the cabin of an outfitter, "Curly" Phillips, with her back toward Edward. Perhaps it is appealing because it is evocative of fairy tales, or maybe children just like animals. Not at all fearsome, Janet was an intelligent German Shepherd dog, "almost like a human being," said Edward. She lived during the 1920s and had been given to Edward as a pup during the filming of a *Strongheart* movie. Indeed, she was an offspring of the canine film star.

Edward and other guides did "stand-in" parts for various actors; Rudolf stood in for John Barrymore. Such work was not only fun but was remunerated at the fantastically high rate of $40 to $45 per day. The exception to fun was the day Edward agreed to carry a Bell & Howell movie camera up Sulphur Mountain, a summit at Banff with a nice trail. The problem was that it was March and there was too much snow on the trail to make it feasible. For this reason, Edward chose to ascend via the ridge (from the Cave and Basin hot springs), but it was still not easy. Sinking up to his knees with almost every step, it was a tremendous amount of work for what turned out to be ten minutes of filming.[60]

When we were younger, we slept on the floor with the bear rug and other animal remnants, as we first had years earlier at Edward's cabin. When we were older, Cindy and I slept on the massive sofa, behind which was a panoramic photograph of the *Berner Oberland*. Singly we could barely budge the sofa, but heaving together we could convert it into a bed of sorts. I say of sorts because the steep slopes created by this antique made it difficult to resist colliding into each other in the middle. We often thought it would have been beneficial to tie-in – a kind of bedroom bivouac – but instead we tried to dangle an arm or a leg over our respective edges, to counteract gravity. Also in the room was a matching chair, equally ponderous, a lovely coffee table Edward had made, and lots of lamps. An ancient gas heater waited ready to flame into service on chilly evenings. This was a basement, after all. An old-fashioned Victrola had possession of one corner of the room. Records were diverse and included popular songs such as "I'll Take You Home Again, Kathleen" (sung in an excessive tremolo style), Strauss waltzes and "Springtime in the Rockies." My favourite was an a cappella Swiss men's chorus – yodelling of course. One wall housed a built-in cabinet. On the top of this were memorabilia from Switzerland (including family portraits) and a large cluster of sparkling crystal quartz.

Cindy and I were allowed to look through items in the cabinet whenever we wanted. There we would find photo albums – black pages with photo corners glued into place and carefully annotated by Martha, who kept records and .was the official correspondent – and scrapbooks filled with articles. There were rows of photographic slides (almost a thousand taken by Edward); books that had been written about Rocky Mountain exploits, some dedicated to and all autographed for Edward; numerous letters; even collections of now "vintage" postcards. But the most precious item there was a small book: his official certification as a guide. The *Führer-Buch*, which, much to our surprise, Edward would eventually ask Cindy and me to sign, contained glowing comments, reminiscences and the recommendations of clients all the way back to his first days as a *Träger* in 1902.

Usually we studied these treasures at bedtime – handling them gently and returning them carefully to their proper places – before drifting off, peaks all around us, into peaceful mountain slumber.

As the years went by and my parents were engaged in a seemingly endless search for a place to retire, Edward suggested they "buy my house." After some stunned surprise that he would suggest such a thing, it became an intriguing idea. Assured that he really meant it, and having researched a fair market price, Pat bought the house, with the proviso that Edward, who was looking forward to the bustle of a busy household, would have a lifetime right to tenancy. And so it was that the keys to Feuz Haus were eventually given to us, and in turn Edward handed the sale proceeds directly to his daughters.

CHAPTER 6

HOW THEY DID IT

To city dwellers who associated "somewhere" with buildings, it was no doubt a source of much puzzlement – after a series of loud *thunks* and a roar of escaping steam – to find the train stopped. The pungent odour of coal mixed with steam reached the nostrils as billowing clouds settled around the train. "Where are we?" travellers asked. Then, from one of the cars, a small party could be seen emerging – hobnail boots on their feet, rucksacks on their backs, each clutching a wooden-shafted ice axe. Interrupting their repose, card games and tea, passengers scurried across the aisle and craned their necks for a better view. Conversation turned toward speculation. With a loud bang and a lurching motion, the train began grinding forward again, leaving the escapees behind to be absorbed by the seemingly endless green forest.

It is no wonder that some have argued that the Canadian psyche was, at least at some point in the past, inextricably connected to the forest in a relationship of awe similar to that of northern Europeans, people whose ancestors were animists. The woods were fearsome and mysterious places: dense and dark, easy to get lost in, the homes of tree spirits, the places that evoked fairy tales. Forests were not perceived as distant velvety carpets, an impression one might get from flying over them. Rather, they were entered into as a realm unto themselves, where the difference between the sizes of their individual members and ours is obvious. If trees are not merely seen as barriers to be overcome to achieve one's goal of reaching the alpine, and we take the time to absorb what is around us, we can still feel the forest's lingering mystery. When walking amongst stands of especially large trees, Edward, without comment, or self-consciousness, always removed his hat.

Travelling by train is how guides and their parties sometimes found themselves in the vicinity of a reasonable starting point when the object of interest was not within walking distance from the hotel. More often there were seemingly endless slogs alongside the tracks, occasionally to be covered in soot by a passing train. Once in the trees there was plenty of bushwhacking, until some trails were built (although trails were never built *everywhere*), and travellers were always grateful to find evidence of animal trails heading in the general direction they wished to go, or old trappers' blazes on trees to guide them. Certainly, Edward wearied of the heavy bush, especially along "steep side hills" which could be thick with alder and devil's club. Flourishing in old growth forest, devil's club is a nasty plant with abundant spines. After repeated, unavoidable contact with this well-defended species, it was not uncommon for his hands to bleed.

Overnight trips could entail carrying everything needed on one's back and sleeping under the stars – or perhaps in a makeshift shelter or small tent – and for some trips, hiring an outfitter, such as the renowned Jimmy Simpson.

Justin James McCarthy Simpson was born in England in 1877. Sent to Canada in 1896 for his wayward nature, he became a trapper, guide, outfitter and lodge owner. Although he did not talk much about his former life in the Old Country, it is easy to intuit Simpson's family status from the fact that his ancestors had been given a family crest. His father was an amateur antiquarian, and Jimmy himself had attended Stamford School. We are told further that on his exile to Canada, he wore a new suit stuffed with sovereigns and adorned with a gold watch and chain.[61] People from all social classes found themselves yielding to the call of the mountains. The gentleman outfitter was not at all unique.

Outfitters and horse guides like Jimmy Simpson (along with their packers) who worked with the Swiss guides arranged for tents and provisions to be transported – frequently by horseback but not always – to spots deemed suitable for a basecamp. In thicker bush and forest, they often had to cut a trail as they went. It was hard work for the packers, time-consuming and no doubt boring as well. Longer expeditions could be quite extravagant by today's standards, sometimes requiring a string of horses and frequently employing a cook.

Although most packers were more than competent, a series of misjudgments while on a trip in a remote area of British Columbia in 1911 resulted in Edward and his party being "starved," having endured three strenuous days without food. Thankfully they were able to find berries on the return trip which gave them enough energy – barely – to somehow keep plodding along.

The packer, although desperately hungry, had stubbornly refused to eat any berries. Upon hearing a distant whistle, he acquired a sudden jolt of motivation and despite his weakened state, expressed a desire to go ahead and catch the train. Edward, although skeptical, assented, saying he *should* go if he felt he could. Sometime later they found the poor fellow face down on the trail, moaning that he was too hungry and "done in" to go on. With much coaxing, which escalated to firmly being told he simply had to do it, the man ate some berries and began making his way slowly downward with the rest of the party.

Once they reached the tracks, Edward, being quite adept at procedures required to produce loud noises, set a "torpedo" to stop the train. The switchman, who knew Edward, welcomed the exhausted and dishevelled party aboard. And when the conductor began to chastise them for stopping the train, the switchman leapt to their defence exclaiming, "These are the mountaineers!"

Provisions generally were heavy, consisting of tins and sacks of this and that. So were the pots and pans, various cooking implements and other equipment such as tents made of canvas. Alas, in the early days there were no sleeping bags, let alone foam pads or light, compact and easy to inflate air mattresses. Mary Vaux,* an adventurer

* Mary Vaux (1860–1940), a Quaker, was the daughter of George Vaux VIII of Philadelphia. She arrived with her father and two brothers (George and William) at the newly opened Glacier House in 1887 and eventually would make over 40 trips to the Canadian mountains.

and amateur scientist, speaking in 1907, advised that "to begin with, a good tent is required, plenty of warm blankets, and a canvas sheet to be spread under and over the blankets on the bough-bed, to prevent dampness from above and below"[62]

Once the tent is pitched and the beds assembled, and it is time to settle in for the night, it is wise to remember that animals, of sundry species, can be a hazard to one's most essential gear. "Always bring your boots into the tent with you. The porkies [porcupines] like the salt and will chew on them," Edward explained, sounding sympathetic to the porkies. What he did not reveal to us, probably because it was an embarrassing cautionary tale, was that he had once left a brand-new pair of boots on a log overnight.

The year was 1903, Edward's very first season in Canada. He had gone to Emerald Lake, a pleasant Swiss-like lodge, which he approved of, with a student on summer break who wanted to climb Mount Habel (now called Mont des Poilus). The next day, they set up camp near Whisky-jack Creek. The boots were left on a log when the party of two retired for the night. The following morning, Edward experienced a *what's wrong with this picture?* moment when he realized that one of his boots was quite a distance from the log. Closer inspection revealed more than minor mischief. The whole side of the boot had been chewed out. He couldn't climb. He couldn't go anywhere. The only solution was to send the student back over Yoho Pass to fetch another pair of boots, a delay which, much to Edward's disgust, wasted a whole day.[63]

Six years later, feeling too warm after a quick hike on a sunny day, Edward removed his "slick, light-coloured" English tweed jacket. It was a favourite, custom-made for him by a London tailor. He folded it neatly, placed it atop a large boulder and went to assess conditions at Abbot Pass. When he returned, there was no jacket. He was absolutely certain he was at the right boulder. Muttering a few appropriate Swiss phrases, he scanned the environment with annoyance, thinking someone must have taken it. But there was no one to be seen. The only plausible scenario he could imagine was that a marmot family, much to the envy of the entire neighbourhood, had lavishly redecorated their den with the finest English tweed.[64]

When packhorses were used for excursions, it was possible to transport a great many supplies (even extra boots) along with provisions. Bacon seemed to be a dietary essential in the old days, probably because it was cured and tasted good. Many an early explorer would rapturously describe the olfactory delights of wood smoke and sizzling bacon. Jam and bacon sandwiches appear to have been *de rigueur*. Not surprisingly, non-human inhabitants of the forest also succumbed to the allure of bacon sizzling, sometimes presenting themselves as unexpected dinner guests.

The aforementioned Mary Vaux begins her list of recommended supplies of food and foodstuffs with bacon and also includes "ham, tea, coffee, evaporated cream, butter, oatmeal, rice, beans, flour, canned tomatoes, canned soup, onions, potatoes, pickles, marmalade, cheese and dried fruits." She goes on to add charmingly that [these] "can be so prepared that with *hunger sauce* [my italics], there is nothing left to be desired in the way of a larger bill of fare." However, she ruins her credibility by adding, "Trout and game are always a welcome addition to the larder."[65]

It was not infrequent on expeditions to encounter large rivers that needed to be forded on horseback, sometimes accompanied by as many as two dozen pack animals. Walter Wilcox related some of the difficulties encountered on these fords:

> As the saddle-horses are guided by riders, they rarely lose their footing, but the pack-animals, coming along in a bunch, confused by the shouting of the men and the roar of the rapids, hesitate and often enter the river a little above or below the best ford, and so get into deep water. Dangerous rapids or a log jam below make such occasions critical, not alone for the safety of the horse, but even for the success of an expedition in case a large quantity of provisions is lost. Pack-horses cannot swim very far with their tight cinches; and moreover the icy waters of these mountains paralyse their muscles very quickly.[66]

The poor horse certainly worked hard in the service of humans. Though not an enthusiastic horseman, Edward nevertheless had a sympathetic attitude toward the plight of this animal. Once while he was walking behind a string of pack horses as they travelled beside the

North Saskatchewan River, the last horse slipped into the torrent. As the horse was carried away, Edward fought to keep from breaking down in tears, and murmured to himself, "Goodbye, little pony." This particular little pony turned out to be very lucky. An hour or so later, while Edward and the others were drying themselves off from their own plunge, he was overjoyed to see the little horse scrambling back up the bank![67]

Now largely a thing of the past, the pack train was a tough way to travel. Nevertheless, it was romanticized even in its day. Writing in 1911, Elizabeth Parker* enthused:

> May the day never come in the Selkirks when the pack-train will cease... A day of such travel in the cool penetralia of these almost tropical forests is better than a thousand by luxurious utilitarian ways of transit. To a healthy soul, its very discomforts are enjoyable and preferable to the conveniences of the private car.[68]

Eventually, overnight huts were built in a few strategic locations, and horses helped make this possible. Many of the huts were small and made of logs, such as the old Hermit Hut (the first built by the CPR) across the valley from Glacier House. Gradually a series of rather grand log huts were built by the Alpine Club of Canada, the first having been completed in 1927.

* Elizabeth Parker (1856–1944) was a Winnipeg journalist and co-founder of the Alpine Club of Canada. The club named a hut for her at Lake O'Hara.

But the most aesthetically pleasing of all the huts and until recently the highest habitable structure in Canada – the one at Abbot Pass – was constructed of stone. The guides were tired of leading guests up and down Mount Victoria in a single day and wanted to make the climb easier and "more enjoyable" for them. Abbot Pass was the ideal location for an alpine hut. Edward and Rudolf, used to high climbing huts in Switzerland, knew what they wanted. Putting their heads together they made some drawings and approached the construction foreman for the CPR, Basil Gardom, with their sketches. "He took things in hand," said Edward. This meant he badgered the CPR until architectural plans were made. The badgering was successful, because construction was begun and completed in 1922, at a cost of $35,000. Gardom had become a helpful ally to Edward and Rudolf, and they were grateful to him.

Although the location was perfect for people wanting to climb Mount Victoria, or Mount Lefroy, getting the project built was strategically difficult and labour-intensive. Pack horses carried construction materials and hut furnishings up the glacier about halfway to the pass, at a point where there was a large crevasse. Even getting that far was not completely without hazard. In one instance, a rockslide tumbled from above, swamping the horses with rubble partway up their legs. After the slide, Edward cajoled the understandably nervous packer, who was refusing to proceed, with, "Don't be frightened; you haven't lost anything," meaning the horses had not been injured. With continued gentle persuasion, Edward was able to convince the still hesitant packer to continue leading his horses up the glacier.* Although, having been buried up to their hocks, one assumes the horses were skittish too.

Once they reached the crevasse, the horses were unloaded. The guides themselves carried the materials on their backs, crossing the crevasse on a ladder they had made. From there the loads were placed on a large sleigh with a strong crossbar and with skis for runners, also made specifically for this project. Two men winched the materials-laden sleigh to the top of the pass. Edward estimated that the cumulative weight of the loads, carried and winched, was almost two tons.

The new hut was officially opened for the 1923 climbing season. But on October 30, 1922, Edward wrote to J. Monroe Thorington, "I enclose a [photo] of Abbot Pass Hut, which is finished now; and think you would be quite interested. Was up on skis yesterday, Oct. 29th, but it was a hard trip."

A trip of several weeks to the Columbia Icefields region in 1924, which included an outfitter/chef, Max Brooks, and two packers, Eric Stanton and Cecil Smith, is a good example of how ambitious horse-supported climbing expeditions could be. The Swiss guides on the trip were Edward, and Joseph Biner from Zermatt, who had never previously climbed in Canada. The clients were the brothers Osgood and Fred Field (Vanderbilts on their mother's side), and a friend, Lem Harris. The goal, proposed enthusiastically by Osgood, was to climb a high

---

* Unfortunately, in a separate incident during construction of the hut, a horse did lose its life when it fell into a crevasse.

mountain called the South Twin (3580 metres) for the first time. The nearby North Twin (3730 metres) had already been climbed. The expedition necessitated extensive travelling on horseback* north from Lake Louise and fording some large rivers. Unfortunately for Biner, who had never ridden before, it was a steep learning curve. A one point, a packer came alongside Edward and asked, "What is he doing?" referring to Biner. Turning to look, Edward saw a small, black speck far behind them in the river. Furthermore, the speck appeared to be stationary. Edward rode back to Biner and asked in Swiss, "What are you doing? Aren't you coming?" Biner, apparently dizzy and confused by the swift current swirling around him, responded, "Oh, I thought I was."[69]

Eventually, they did make it to their basecamp at Castleguard Meadows and spent the next few days conditioning on less demanding climbs. Leaving their support team and horses behind, the guides and their clients set off at eight o'clock at night on July 8 to begin the 12 miles (19 kilometres) of glacier travel to reach the South Twin, where they would climb through the night. Their biggest challenge occurred high up on the ridge of the peak where they encountered a wind so strong that they were forced to crawl on hands and knees. Nevertheless, they reached the summit at eight o'clock in the morning, thus achieving the first ascent.

Descending to the col (or pass) between the two peaks, and buoyed by their success on the previous Twin, the

* About six days.

group of five decided to proceed upward again, and thus became the second party to climb the North Twin. But after descending the second mountain the jubilant climbers still had the 19-kilometre slog back to basecamp ahead of them. Some members of the party became so fatigued during the tedious march – which would complete a 24-hour grand tour – that they fell asleep on their feet; others experienced what can only be described as visual hallucinations. Trees and shrubs do not grow on glaciers!

After a two-day rest they climbed Mount Castleguard near their camp, and the following day they completed a new route (along the south ridge) of the massive and wearying Mount Columbia (3737 metres). Also along for the latter climb were the two packers and the outfitter, all novices, who after their success were united in the opinion that one mountaineering experience was enough for a lifetime.

On the way home, still eager for more, the Field brothers and Edward climbed several other peaks before making their way to Mount Patterson. Getting there entailed travelling south along the Mistaya River for 14 miles (around 22.5 kilometres) by horse and setting up another camp. However, having done so, they still had the barrier of a large, frigid lake between themselves and their goal.

As a child, I was enamoured of the adventures of the fictional Tom Sawyer and Huckleberry Finn. So the solution to the problem of the lake was far more thrilling to me than the ascent of the mountain, the name of which I had forgotten over the years. They did indeed build rafts. After poling for three miles (five kilometres) they camped for the night on the south side of Mistaya Lake – obviously no mere puddle. The ascent of the mountain the next morning would have required an altitude gain of 4,875 feet (1486 metres), which they were able to achieve in six hours. After enjoying spectacular and wide-ranging views on this peak, they spent another six hours descending, and after another Tom Sawyer/Huckleberry Finn enactment, returned to their original camp on the Mistaya River.

The entirety of their ambitious and successful expedition – during which they climbed a total of eight peaks over 10,000 feet high, five of which were first ascents – was later described as "what is possible only for young and energetic climbers."[70] While it was true that all three clients were 20 years old or younger, Edward was twice that age and Joseph Biner was even older.

While many early climbs did not necessitate expeditions, single-day outings shorter than 24-hour hallucination-inducing marathon efforts can still be arduous. Edward found stopping for tea in the afternoon, even in hot weather, to be a restorative break; in cold weather the appeal is obvious. He would boil water over a small fire, toss in some tea – loose or in tea bags – and "cook" it for a while. Pouring the brew into cups placed on a relatively flat rock, he would then add lumps of sugar and leave the mixture to cool down a little, because hot metal cups are hard to handle and hard on the lips. Edward did have a vintage brass Primus expedition-type stove which he frequently brought along on overnight trips which were not supported by packers. On a day trip a stove would usually be declared unnecessary and deemed to be too much weight to add to an old-fashioned rucksack.

Rucksacks could be mail-ordered from the old country or made to specification by the local harness maker in Golden, Mr. Wenman. They were mostly made of canvas of various thicknesses. Unlike the sophisticated designs of packs today, which distribute weight through the hips, rucksacks were not much more elaborate than just that: sacks, with all the weight hanging from one's shoulders. When climbing, rucksacks would tend to shift on one's back, so that you might find yourself manoeuvring it into a more centred position by shifting your shoulders or pushing it with your hand, if one were available at the time.

Into the rucksack went sundry items, but certainly food, a metal water flask (Edward's held about a half-litre), matches, extra clothing, a slicker (rain poncho) and first aid supplies as well as field glasses, a compass and a camera. There were no radios, let alone cell phones or global positioning systems. If you were lost or stuck on a ledge somewhere, you could only stay there and wait, hopefully to be rescued.

An early, and now famous, rescue attempt occurred in 1921 when two climbers from the Alpine Club of Canada jubilee encampment at Mount Assiniboine set off to make a first ascent attempt on the nearby Mount Eon. In an ironic twist, one member of the party had just written an article in defence of amateur climbing.[71] It should be said that although Edward believed it was reckless to venture up a mountain without the requisite skills, he was in no way opposed to amateur mountaineering. One of the roles of the guide, he felt, in relation to interested amateurs, was that of a mentor and teacher. He would often show young people the way up a mountain, and sent my sister and me off to climb peaks on our own.

Nevertheless, the 1921 accident shocked and saddened the whole mountaineering community, amateur and professional alike. Winthrop E. Stone, Ph.D., LL.D., president of Purdue University, was leading the way up a chimney, near the summit of the mountain, while his wife, Margaret, waited below, belaying him on a ledge. He emerged from the top of the chimney and then disappeared from his wife's sight.

A.H. MacCarthy narrates what happened next:

> ... without any warning, a large slab of rock tumbled off from above, passing over Mrs. Stone, and was closely followed by Dr. Stone, who spoke no word but held his ice axe firmly in his right hand. Horror stricken at the sight, Mrs. Stone braced herself to take the jerk of the rope...[72]

No jerk followed. Dr. Stone had untied himself from the rope.

Once it was realized that the pair were overdue from their expedition – of course, no one had any idea what had happened – search parties were assembled and launched but they received no reward for their efforts. Hence, Swiss guides were summoned.

In the interim, an immensely distraught Mrs. Stone

made attempts to descend the mountain on her own but was unable to do so, ultimately finding herself trapped on a ledge. By the time she was found, she was too weak to walk, let alone climb, and was carried down the mountain on the back of the leader, Rudolf Aemmer, using a technique he had learned in his guide training. In Ruedi's own words, "I carried her for 4½ hours on my back. I cut some rope, made a sling in which Mrs. Stone could sit and also large enough to get my shoulders in; with another rope I tied her to myself; that gave me the arms free for holds and the use of the ice-axe."[73]

After the rescue of Margaret Stone a second party consisting of three guides, Rudolph, Edward and Conrad Kain (an Austrian guide) along with amateurs Lennox Lindsay and A.H. MacCarthy, was assembled to search for the cause of the accident, as they assumed Dr. Stone had not survived his fall. The party, led by Edward, retraced the probable ascent route on the mountain. He spotted the body immediately below the summit. Soon afterward Kain found the ice axe Dr. Stone had been gripping as he flew past his wife, plunging to his death. The search party deduced that having disappeared from view and untied himself from the rope, he had achieved the summit, thus having completed the first ascent of the mountain. Tragically, he had subsequently slipped on loose rock as he was making his way back down to the chimney.

After building a cairn and planting Dr. Stone's ice axe on the summit, the grisly task of recovering the body ensued. It took the team from five in the morning until one in the afternoon to lower the body off the mountain.[74] In regard to the whole recovery operation, MacCarthy remarked that "Conrad, Edward and Rudolph did heroic work on that perilous mountain side..."[75]

Years after the accident, Edward continued to have the greatest sympathy for Margaret Stone and respect for her toughness in the face of the ordeal she had undergone. For eight long days she was exposed to the elements, stranded on the mountain, not knowing if she would be rescued. Despondent, without food, and dressed in only a flannel shirt and knickers, she might not have survived had she not been fortunate enough to have found a small trickle of water that helped sustain her.

In order to be prepared for the unpredictable, Edward counselled, "Always take a little extra grub – a tin of sardines." This last bit of advice, which was repeated often, tended to elicit a slight shudder from some of my relatives. Sardines are not mentioned explicitly in Mary Vaux's list of foods, but no doubt this was a popular item for the early mountaineer due to its nutritional appeal, absence of spoilage and convenience of size – it could be crammed into one's rucksack no matter how full, as an emergency food item.

The Stone party had shared a rucksack, which was on Dr. Stone's back when he fell. This left his wife with no jacket, though her shirt could have been wool flannel, which would have kept her warmer than if she had been wearing mere cotton flannel.

Edward often wore a cotton flannel shirt, but he always had his wool suit jacket with him, and for higher climbs he would also bring a sweater. Wool was bulky but it was warm even when wet and thus was used in trousers, jackets, toques, gloves and so forth. Interestingly, we are now coming full circle, with merino wool (lighter and easily washed) being touted as superior to synthetic fibres (which do wick but frankly can be fairly foul smelling) for base layers and shirts. Knickers (knee-length trousers, not underwear) with long woollen socks were better for climbing because they made it easier to bend one's knees (as when stepping upward), whereas full-length trousers would bind.

Covering one's legs completely is sensible, as it offers some protection from minor scrapes and is practical for travelling into high terrain, where the weather can be much cooler than down in the valleys and conditions can change very quickly to produce unpleasant scenarios such as snow. In the early days, "ladies" still wore long skirts and impossible shoes. Edward soon persuaded those he climbed with to switch to knee-length trousers and socks, not only for their own benefit but because skirts dragging on scree had the unfortunate consequence of knocking down lots of rock on climbers below. As for those impossible shoes, switching to real mountaineering boots was just common sense.

Felt hats afforded climbers protection from the sun. Glacier goggles – designed to prevent snow blindness – had protruding tin frames with slightly oval-shaped smoked-glass lenses, giving the wearer a decidedly odd, bug-like appearance. For the converse situation of not enough light, modern climbers use small battery-powered headlamps for making an early start or climbing in the dark. In earlier times, they would have needed a free hand to carry a small collapsible lantern with a candle in it. If a breeze came up...

Besides specialized clothing, though, the most important piece of equipment for the traditional mountaineer was the ice axe. Useful in all sorts of situations, although sometimes awkward, it was eminently more practical on steep terrain than a walking stick or thin hiking poles (ski-style). The ice axe is sturdier. The shaft, typically made of ash, has greater girth and is far superior for across-the-body techniques. In other words, the iron-pointed walking-stick end can be planted on the upside of the slope for traversing tricky sections. It is also useful for glissading. The latter is a fun technique akin to skiing on one's feet and is used to travel quickly on "safe snow," that is, where there is no threat of sliding into a crevasse or crashing into rocks when the snow has run out. The ice axe also has two additional useful features on the "handle" end: an adze, and opposite it a pick with a serrated edge. The adze is designed for cutting steps in snow or ice, while the pick is essential for self-arrest (or arresting a companion) should there be a slip on steep snow or ice.

Initially ice axes were quite long, having evolved from the alpenstock. By the old standard they should be long enough to use as a walking stick – that is, as a third point of balance – and should have enough heft to be useful in chopping steps. A more recent guide for gauging the proper length of an ice axe relative to one's own body size is to hold it upright with its pointed end on the ground and raise one's leg to rest the bend of the knee on the axe head. In that position, one's thigh should be parallel to the ground. If the thigh is slanted slightly upward, the axe is too long, or conversely too short if one's thigh is slanted downward.

The wooden shafts of the old ice axes would develop an attractive patina over time. Today, the alpine ice axe, entirely made of metal, is no longer a thing of beauty. It is also now too short to use on all but very steep slopes. The modern mountaineer looks silly, to my mind, carrying an axe the point of which dangles feet from the nearest solid surface.

As J. Monroe Thorington* described travel on a large glacier in the Freshfield group in 1922, it is easy to imagine how they might be using their ice axes not only to chop steps but as a third point of balance:

> We were soon in a labyrinth of crevasses, which we threaded, cutting steps, or crossing by firm snowbridges from which hung shining icicles that dripped water into blue depths and darkness. No sounds save the bell-like tinkle of water dripping against the ice, and the faint whisper of an early morning breeze sweeping up the slopes – a near-silence broken by Edward, admonishing us to walk like cats and by no means to jump on the snow-bridges. There were places where we balanced like acrobats,

---

* J. Monroe Thorington (1894–1989) was a Princeton graduate and Philadelphia ophthalmologist. He wrote *The Glittering Mountains of Canada* and, with Howard Palmer, *A Climber's Guide to the Rocky Mountains of Canada*.

on the crests – Edward dubbed them "garden-walls" – between two crevasses. Huge things those crevasses were: some nearly a hundred feet wide...[76]

Earlier, recounting the first ascent of Mount Sir Sandford, in 1912, Howard Palmer wrote this description of Edward negotiating an open crevasse:

> It was too wide to reach across with an axe, so Feuz, after selecting a soft-looking place on the farther side, executed a neat flying leap and landed safely on all fours. The rest of us then followed his example, not without secret misgiving, I fear, as to the procedure to be employed in getting back later, for the side we had just left was considerably higher.[77]

What Palmer meant by "too wide to reach across with an axe" is that normally one would approach the edge of a crevasse, checking to ensure it was safe, of course, and then reach across the gap with the ice axe, using the walking stick end of it to probe the snow on the other side to ascertain whether it too was safe. Then the axe, its walking stick end having been stuck into the snow or balanced on the ice, would help the climber maintain balance and stability when stepping or jumping over the gap.

On the return trip Edward used a technique to gain a little height on his leap back across the crevasse, which, as Palmer correctly inferred, required jumping uphill. "The wide crevasse," Palmer tells us, "yielded to a skilful spring by Feuz using Aemmer's knee as a take off."[78]

Mountaineering hobnail boots were made of leather

(the laces were leather as well) with metal cleats (or nails) pounded into the soles. Needless to say, boots in those days were heavy – Edward's weighed four pounds each. But weight is not always a bad thing. Boots are a lot like tires on a vehicle: a heavy-duty version is more appropriate for rough terrain. And a heavier boot is helpful for "heeling down" in deep snow. Hobnail boots had great utility on snow and ice due to their built-in grip, and they did not slip on wet rock the way Vibram-soled boots do. Those who climbed in them frequently claimed they did not slip on steeper rock. If you did not know the route, you could follow little scratch marks made by the nails of others' boots – with the proviso that it is not always wise to follow the paths others leave.

On an especially steep section of rock, Edward would occasionally exchange his heavy footgear for a pair of canvas (running-type) shoes with rope (and later rubber) soles, and probably more than once he climbed in his socks. Modern, ballet-like climbing shoes with sticky rubber soles are an obvious quantum leap forward on steep rock that has small to non-existent toeholds. One's own personal capacities are enhanced by switching from boots to climbing shoes, and they vastly expand the range of steep rock that is climbable.

Despite changes in equipment, the rudiments of climbing, the skilful use of hand and foot placements to move upward on glaciated or steep rocky terrain – and then of course, down again – is basically unchanged. There are some techniques which have fallen out of fashion, most would say thankfully. For example,

The *shoulder stand* or *human ladder*, still sometimes called by the French term of *courte échelle*, is used to overcome a holdless lower section of a pitch, in order to reach the easier climbing above… the lower man should be well secured so that he can maintain his position even against an unexpected push. He will find it more comfortable if he has on a coat and hat, *especially if the leader is climbing in nails* [latter italics mine].[79]

On what was to be the first ascent of Mount Saint Bride (previously called White Douglas), Edward's father (Edward Sr.) apparently felt it necessary to take a ladder with him, and he set about preparing a reasonable substitute by cutting down a tree. He thought the tree-cum-ladder would be helpful in ascending a difficult chimney he had encountered on an earlier attempt on the mountain. The party started off on relatively easy terrain, "although the tree was something of a drag," as their client, Joseph Hickson,* reported.[80]

During a steep, snow-covered glacial detour, the party had to descend backwards for 500 feet (about 150 metres). In other words, facing inwards (toward the slope) they kicked the toes of their boots into the slope as they moved downward. Remarking about this detour, Hickson said, with some understatement, "Edward (Jr.)

---

* Joseph William Andrew Hickson (1873–1956), son of Sir Joseph Hickson, was a professor of philosophy and psychology at McGill University. A keen mountaineer despite a deformed leg resulting from having been rolled on by a horse, he made about 30 first ascents with Edward and participated in many other climbs.

had to expend considerable energy as he had latterly assumed the burden of carrying the heavy and useless pole." Edward downclimbing a steep snow slope, using his ice axe in one hand and balancing the pole, presumably on his opposite shoulder, evokes a most disconcerting image.

Once the notorious chimney had finally been reached, and the pole had been dragged or carried 4,000 feet (1219 metres), it was declared inappropriate for ascending the chimney, as it could not be stabilized. Thus ended the saga of the tree which became a pole, never served as a ladder and was unceremoniously abandoned at what was, for the tree, a high altitude.

With no ladder to assist them, the day was saved by Feuz Jr., who after an initial attempt made a second go at the chimney sans artificial assistance. After testing his holds "he pluckily took a chance and made the crucial move, which was successful. By a vigorous pull, during which we were all anxiety, he drew himself into the chimney where, standing for a couple of minutes fairly secure with his face toward its vertical walls, he waved his arm and I felt that Douglas was captured."[81] In later years when he was asked how he had managed this, Edward responded honestly, "I don't know; I couldn't tell you."[82] Hickson goes on to say that the remainder of the chimney was hard, with an overhanging top, which demanded "strong fore-arms and generally good muscles."[83] After this difficult section, the climb was no trouble at all and the top, said Edward, was "big enough for a hotel."

Ropes were and still are used for safety. Edward preferred English ones, which were made of manila hemp (nylon ropes came considerably later). Each year on his trips back to Canada from Switzerland, he bought a new rope on his way through London. Later he was dependent on mail order catalogues. Prior to climbing harnesses, ropes were simply tied around the waist (or chest), usually with a bowline knot. On a taut rope the potential for discomfort is easily imagined.

Using ropes on a rock climb secured everyone who followed, but securing the leader was virtually impossible. All the second climber in line could do was hang on as the leader fell past. So, in the description above, of Edward leading on Douglas, he had no real protection from a fall, while his father, being roped and in this case climbing second, would have had an easier time.

J. Monroe Thorington, on the ascent of Nanga Parbat (in the Freshfield group) with Howard Palmer, related what he felt was a humorous incident, but perhaps it was less so for Palmer: "I was the middle man on the rope and Palmer [a large man] last – Edward having jokingly remarked that he wanted a good anchor on the end, in case he should unexpectedly plumb the depths of a crevasse…"[84] Belaying the leader is somewhat different today, as we will see below, although it is never a bad idea to have a substantial anchor on the end of the rope.

Climbers would rope up when the terrain became more difficult and there was no trail. Guides would take no chances with guests on very steep scree or when there were rocky ledges to be successfully scrambled over. In more dangerous situations, the whole party would move together, but the guest would be on a short rope. The reason for this is that on a short rope, a slip is more likely to stay a slip and not develop into a fall. Think of controlling a big, rambunctious dog on steep terrain with a long leash versus a short one. To make the image clearer, and more frightening, imagine the dog on its long leash is behind you. Any unexpected jerk on a taut rope could easily pull you off your feet.

In other circumstances, such as on a low-angled snow field, everyone on the rope would move together, at equal distance from each other. In the event of a slip, the guide (or guides) would work quickly to secure themselves and tighten the rope, to avoid a serious accident – someone sliding or falling down the slope uncontrollably, perhaps into a crevasse or over a cliff.

In the case of a serious slip on an ice field, the point of the ice axe would be jammed firmly into the snow vertically. Simultaneously, a loop of rope would be thrown around the adze in order to secure one's position and in theory resist the force of a falling body. Sometimes it would be necessary to then throw oneself face down on the snow while sliding one's hands down the shaft of the axe to decrease the chance of the axe being pulled out. Spreading one's legs and kicking one's toes into the snow creates a more stable surface, provided one is not wearing crampons, as the spiky points on those otherwise useful devices would only make matters worse in this type of situation. This manoeuvre is similar to a self-arrest, except in the latter case the pick portion of the axe is jammed into the snow or ice.

Speed and timing are also of the essence. My father

had a vivid pictorial memory of a loop of rope in the air, framing the clear blue sky, just as he was jerked off his feet by his partner, simultaneously losing his grip on his axe. He and his friend and fellow CPR employee Arthur Oldfield tumbled head over heels, stopping only at the toe of the glacier. Sitting in the snow dazed and still tied together, they stared in disbelief at the seemingly tiny ice axe still firmly planted and standing like a sentinel far above them. They knew they had been lucky.

Mount Victoria is a beautiful climb. It has a long, relatively narrow summit ridge along the Great Divide, which offers the reward of sustained and spectacular views. Everyone wanted to climb it, as it was the central focus from the Chateau's huge picture windows. Certainly, each individual guide had ascended it a hundred times or more in his career. One season, growing weary from so many requests to climb the mountain, Ernst declared, with some creative licence, that the route in the pass was not negotiable. This, he explained to his fellow guides, was due to a crevasse which had opened up and become an impassable barrier to ascent of the mountain. This announcement gave Ernst a full climbing season without having to ascend this particular mountain even once. Late in the season, Edward yielded to the persistent entreaties of a guest and went to investigate the situation more fully. He did find a large open crevasse, as expected. The impassable part was somewhat exaggerated, though. Rather than cross the crevasse, Edward found a way to circumvent it entirely by climbing on the side of the mountain above it.

The protocol for a slip and fall on the summit ridge of Mount Victoria is unnerving to most, given the impressive drop-off on both sides of the ridge. The approved technique in such a situation is to throw oneself over the opposite side of the ridge to which one's rope mate has unexpectedly descended, to stop them and prevent oneself from following along. So, if one's partner falls toward Lake Louise (in Alberta), the proper response is to leap into British Columbia, or if one prefers, in the general direction of Lake O'Hara. Fortunately, I personally have no intimate knowledge as to what comes next, supposing one were able to follow through with this suicide-like act.

When a stationary climber secures and monitors the rope for a partner who is climbing, this is called a belay. The point of a belay is to ensure the person climbing does not fall and if they do, to stop them. When the guides belayed a client, they kept the rope quite taut so they could quickly rectify a slip or, if need be, haul the person up. Historically, belays involved techniques which would seem frightening today, such as feeding the rope around one's shoulders or hips, or simply holding the rope in a standing position. In a sitting belay, one can brace one's feet up against a nice solid rock. In trickier situations, there might be additional safety precautions such as feeding the rope through a sling placed over the horn of a stable rock. Nevertheless, security rather than fear was the feeling of the day when being belayed by a guide. Joseph Hickson, referring to Edward and Rudolph, wrote:

But there is practically no danger... when one is firmly held on the rope by guides... whose caution and resourcefulness, here as elsewhere, were admirable, and [who] have fully justified the confidence which I have always reposed in their ability[85]

On a snowfield or glacier, the belayer's ice axe would be shoved deep into the snow, with the rope looped around the adze to be fed through or taken in, depending on whether the belayed climber is ascending or descending. The belayer can also use a feature on the glacier to secure himself, an example of which W.S. Jackson gives in his description of Edward belaying him on a glacier in the Selkirks. Jackson sets the scene by telling us he was instructed to descend diagonally down a steep snow slope, but he is apprehensive. He goes on to say:

[Edward] anchored himself in the edge of [a] little bergschrund, and I started gingerly to kick steps in the slope. I have always hated unstable snow, and my hatred was soon justified. After a dozen steps, the surface began to slide and I with it, until the rope tightened and swung me clear underneath Edward. The breath was almost squeezed out of me, but I hung on to my axe and was soon on the edge of the bergschrund[86]

Approaching gingerly may or may not have been the best way to proceed in this situation, and Jackson's having "always hated unstable snow" may have added to a certain tentativeness in his footwork. Still, descending diagonally on a steep snow slope with just boots (no crampons) can feel very precarious. Nevertheless, despite Jackson's exciting pendulum swing – and subsequent hauling back to his starting point – he survived unscathed to tell the tale of this first ascent. The belay, which entailed Edward first securing himself by using a glacial feature, basically a shallow crack in the ice, had worked.

Nowadays, belaying on rock entails first securing oneself to the cliff by tying the rope into carabiners (specialized metal shackles with spring-loaded gates) which are clipped into permanent or removable metal rings fastened to the rock. In the case of snow, a technique similar to the one used by Edward in the above example might be employed, or, on a longer pitch or on steeper ice, an ice screw (or similar device) can be used. Suffice to say that modern belays, for the most part, are much safer than the old-fashioned ones, which relied on careful attention, quick reactions and sometimes brute strength.

At times when there was a danger that the leader could fall, the "tourist" would be instructed to untie from the rope, because if the leader did fall, there was a good chance he would pull the tourist off the mountain with him. But this would only be done if the tourist could stand, or preferably sit, in a place fairly well protected from the hazard presented by the potentially falling guide – a blasphemous thought – as well as from any rockfall. And, on more dangerous or difficult climbs, two guides were employed, one on each end of the rope, to maximize safety. Two guides could keep the herd together better and monitor developing scenarios. They could also belay each other in tricky situations. Plus, they had an almost foolproof method of secret communication – the Swiss dialect – which allowed them to plot and strategize without interference.

Leaders today can leave some protection for themselves on rock by placing specialized gear in cracks as they go, to run rope through. Gear placement is a little more complicated of course, but this is the gist. The theory is that if the leader falls, they will be arrested by the gear they have placed behind them, so long as the person belaying is doing their job of keeping the rope fast, and assuming the gear does not pop out of the rock. While not completely fail-safe, the modern system is a happier scenario than untying from the rope or hoping the second in line can stop your fall by simply hanging on as you fly past them.

The early climbs in Canada need to be considered in their historical context and in light of the equipment and techniques they were using. Many people today are appreciative of the skills that would have been required in the old days of getting clients safely up peaks, many of which had never been climbed before. Edward was proud, and counted himself fortunate, that in all his years of climbing he never had an accident that was induced by human error and none of his clients were ever seriously hurt. Sometimes it is said that this was because he was not climbing on steep terrain, but this is simply not true. Alpine peaks in general offer more frightening opportunities for mishap than modern rock climbing using gear appropriately. Certainly, there were climbs on peaks that today would be considered "scrambles," and privately the guides themselves could be somewhat dismissive of peaks they considered "walk-ups." Still, regardless of the degree of challenge, climbing is an inherently dangerous activity, and it is for this reason Edward felt that all mountains should be approached with respect. Some of the peaks the old guides climbed are daunting even by today's standards, but difficulty was not really the point.

When Edward was asked which peak had been the hardest he had climbed, he sounded confused. "It is difficult to say," he responded. Mountains are so different in makeup and challenges. "On any mountain," he explained, "there is a little bit which is technical, or hard."[87] In a similar fashion, he could never declare which mountain was his favourite; each had its own delights. I don't think many of us could name a favourite either, and we simply find ourselves reciting the virtues of each summit we have climbed. For example, one might single out a specific peak that had some nice face climbing. Others might have a hand traverse; or a most interesting cornice; steep pitches for its "grade"; perfect snow conditions; the best echo – one could go on and on.

We climbed with very little gear, wearing big leather mountaineering boots at a time when some people used large racks of equipment for the same route. While preferring to use more gear today – as it makes climbs eminently safer – we like to think we climbed some of the classic peaks pretty much as Edward did before us, but we were by no means the only ones.

Rudi Gertsch,* who has fond memories of both Edward and his brother Walter, tells a little tale about the old versus the new. In 1997, Abbot Pass Hut became a National Historic Site. Both Rudi and Syd Feuz (Walter's son) were invited to the hut for the celebration. While Syd was to be interviewed the following afternoon, the main celebratory activity was to climb Mount Victoria; this, after all, was the reason why the guides wanted the hut built and worked so hard to see it happen.

That night Rudi and Syd, excited about the climb, decided that they should get up very early the next morning so they could reach the peak and be back to the hut in time for the interview. Syd had brought his Dad's old wooden-shaft ice axe for the climb, so Rudi brought his old ice axe too. Apparently, not everyone thought this was a good idea:

> We got criticized that we shouldn't be using all this old equipment anymore. It was great for decoration but that's about all. There was definitely some "tech-talk" in the cabin that night about the "poly-super-duper material" they are using for all the climbing equipment. Anyway, while they were busy talking about their equipment, Syd and I made plans.[88]

* Gertsch, a third-generation Swiss mountain guide, was born in Wengen in 1945 and came to Canada in 1966. As owner of Purcell Heliskiing, he was instrumental in pushing for a high standard for Canadian mountain guides. In 1972 the Association of Canadian Mountain Guides was the first non-European mountain guide organization to gain international recognition.

Well, they ignored the critics and went to bed early. The next morning they were roped up and on their way to the summit ridge before anyone else had even awakened. On their way down from the peak, they could see the others coming up, but the weather was changing. Rudi remembered,

> By the time we caught up to them, everyone decided to turn around and go home again. So Syd and I, with our [old] equipment, were the only ones who got to the summit that day. The two of us didn't say much. We just chuckled.

Despite doing his best to climb safely, Edward *was* once caught in an avalanche. He had gladly agreed to take some eager "kitchen boys" who wanted to see the hut up to Abbot Pass in exchange for help carrying firewood. Three to four hundred metres behind Edward's party was Rudolf, also with a crew of boys. Alerted to the sounds of a big avalanche, Martha, from her vantage point at the Plain of Six Glaciers teahouse, witnessed a massive amount of snow cascading down into the Death Trap – exactly where she knew her husband was. And Rudolf, who was lower down and not in the avalanche's path, could also envision what had befallen his best pal. He moved forward as quickly as he could, his heart thumping.

Edward, recalling the event, said there was not much forewarning of danger, other than hearing a "terrific roar." Simultaneously "a big white cloud" made it impossible to see what was happening. His instinct was to urge everyone to try to run across to the opposite side of the pass, away from danger, but this was impossible. Most members of the party were flung into the air and had their rucksacks ripped off their backs by the tremendous pressure which preceded the snow. When the snow did come, Edward tried to plant his ice axe, but he too was lifted into the air and was buried standing up with one arm over his head. What had happened to the others, he did not know. He also had no idea how long he was under the snow. He could breathe, but he could not move, as the snow encasing him felt "just like cement," and he knew his small pocket of air would not last forever. While their predicament had been presaged by a roar, now there was only profound silence. Not only did Edward not have thoughts of mortality, he did not remember any thoughts at all. His experience was more sensory: "cement," "silence," with no perception of time and no emotion.

At some point he began hearing… something. Oddly, it sounded like the scratching of a cat. The sound, which persisted, turned out to be one of the boys from his party using his bare hands to dig him out. What Edward did not know at the time was that he had only been found because four of his fingers had been seen protruding from the snow! Once Edward's face was uncovered, he saw a young man kneeling above him, crying. His hands were so cold from digging, he could no longer stand the pain. But Edward's foot was twisted under him and he could not get out on his own and so the young man had to continue digging despite the pain. Once freed, Edward looked around and it appeared, at first glance, that the others had all been buried only shallowly and were alright. One boy had been thrown into rocks and was bleeding but conscious. However, when Edward counted the boys, he realized that one was missing. Scanning the terrain, they finally spied something that looked like a hat between two clumps of ice. Miraculously, there was the missing boy, "just lying there like a priest," under a small amount of snow. With varying degrees of difficulty, they all managed to walk out, despite their injuries. Glancing above their heads, as they left, they saw that the ice looked as if someone had cut it with a knife.[89]

On another occasion, while climbing one of the Ten Peaks at Moraine Lake (possibly a first ascent of Mount Deltaform, as it happened), Edward was struck by a rock about four inches in diameter. He described this incident as the rock falling "*kerplunk*, right smack on top of my head." The blood streamed down his face, but he simply bandaged up his head, put his hat back on and continued to the top. Joseph Hickson related the incident with a more dramatic flair:

> Aemmer, who entered the chimney first and had cleared away most of the rubbish, was well towards its top and waiting for Feuz to follow when, although exercising great caution, he dislodged a good-sized stone, which, crashing down, inflicted a severe wound on the back of Feuz's head... Blood poured down over Feuz's face and neck, and concluding that the climb was at an end I considered only how we could get down again; for Aemmer

could hardly have descended the chimney without assistance. But as soon as the stunning effect of the blow had passed over, Feuz pulled himself together with wonderful grit and pluckily declared that the accident would make no difference; nor did it.[90]

In those days, climbers did not use helmets; those were for miners.

Reaching the summit of a mountain was always a joyful event. Each member of the party would be congratulated on their accomplishment with a handshake by the guide. A new summit was an occasion to build a stone man or cairn (essentially a substantial stack of rocks) to proclaim the achievement. A written record, protected from the elements by a tin or other container, would be deposited in the cairn, to be signed and annotated by all subsequent summiteers. In good weather and with sufficient time, views would be enjoyed and photographs taken. But as Edward often commented, generally the best photos of mountains themselves are those taken from partway up another mountain. Nevertheless, a summit pictorial representation is a pleasant, tangible reminder of one's climb, and summit photos of surrounding peaks are interesting, somewhat like photos taken from a low-flying airplane.

In bad weather, sometimes all one can hope for at the summit is one circuit around the cairn before descending through the clouds. On a nice day, simple picnics would be savoured, yodels would test for summit echoes, pipes would be smoked and even a snooze might be in order. Sometimes comrades would even burst into song. W. Osgood Field recounts such an occasion in 1924:

> There, perched on the summit, we gave way to our exuberant feelings and sang, or rather shouted, the following song made up from some of the more distinguishable phrases of Swiss pathos:

> *Immer langsam, immer langsam,*
> *Immer höher, höher,*
> *Nach dem Gipfel gehen wir,*
> *Höher, höher, höher,*
> *Warum so müde? Es ist nicht so schlecht,*
> *Komme ich ganz schneller?*
> *Alles geht sehr gut!*[91]

> [Always slowly, always slowly.
> Always higher, higher,
> toward the peak we go.
> Higher, higher, higher.
> Why so tired? It is not too bad.
> Am I coming along much faster?
> Everything is going very well!]

ABOVE Edward at age 80 with the author at Abbot Pass.

BELOW Photographing wildflowers near Balu Pass in 1970 with Mike Stephen. PHOTO: PAT STEPHEN, STEPHEN COLLECTION.

ABOVE A 12-year-old Edward (right) standing next to his proud Swiss guide father on the summit of the Jungfrau in 1897. PHOTO: WHYTE MUSEUM OF THE CANADIAN ROCKIES, EDWARD FEUZ FONDS (V200/PD/31/3).

BELOW Glacier House with the truly impressive Illecillewaet Glacier. PHOTO: RICHARD HENRY TRUEMAN; CITY OF VANCOUVER ARCHIVES, CVA 2-57.

ABOVE Some magnificent Selkirk mountains: Uto Peak, Mount Sir Donald and Eagle Peak. PHOTO: WHYTE MUSEUM OF THE CANADIAN ROCKIES, VAUX FAMILY FONDS (V653/NG-376)

BELOW A drawing by A.O. Wheeler of Uto Peak and Mount Sir Donald showing early climbing routes, from volume 2 of *The Selkirk Range*, published in 1905.

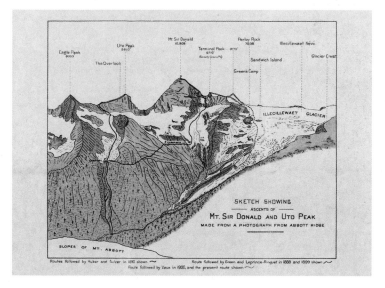

OPPOSITE Finding the way forward on the first ascent of Terminal Peak in 1906. PHOTO: WHYTE MUSEUM OF THE CANADIAN ROCKIES, EDWARD FEUZ FONDS (V200/I/A/II/PA-476).

ABOVE Edward as a young man in Canada. PHOTO: STEPHEN COLLECTION.

OPPOSITE Mount Assiniboine, "Canada's Matterhorn." PHOTO: GEORGE NOBLE; WHYTE MUSEUM OF THE CANADIAN ROCKIES, GEORGE NOBLE FONDS (V469/2838).

ABOVE The iconic Lake Louise with its dramatic backdrop, Mount Victoria. Edward is paddling. PHOTO: NICHOLAS MORANT; BY PERMISSION ACHF/EXPORAIL, CANADIAN PACIFIC RAILWAY COMPANY FONDS (M4953).

LEFT Two lucky guests with a coveted window table at Chateau Lake Louise. PHOTO: WHYTE MUSEUM OF THE CANADIAN ROCKIES, MALCOLM GEDDES FONDS (V756/PS-135).

ABOVE Swiss guides Rudolf Aemmer (top) and his friend Edward Feuz Jr. on the Victoria Glacier. PHOTO: WHYTE MUSEUM OF THE CANADIAN ROCKIES, EDWARD FEUZ FONDS (V200/PB-11).

BELOW A postcard advertising Edelweiss Village. PHOTO: WHYTE MUSEUM OF THE CANADIAN ROCKIES, LIBRARY-POSTCARD SERIES (V66/PG-C63-6-20).

OPPOSITE Mount Sir Sandford, the highest peak in the northern Selkirk mountains and a first ascent in 1912 for Edward, Rudolf, Howard Palmer and E.W.D. Holway. PHOTO: EDWARD FEUZ; STEPHEN COLLECTION.

Portraits of the Swiss guides taken at Guide House, Lake Louise, 1928, by Hans Lüscher. PHOTOS: STEPHEN COLLECTION.

OPPOSITE Edward Feuz

TOP LEFT Ernst Feuz

TOP RIGHT Walter Feuz

BOTTOM LEFT Rudolf Aemmer

BOTTOM RIGHT Christian Häsler

ABOVE Gertie and Hedye Feuz in their Swiss outfits at the teahouse, with Mitre Peak and Mount Lefroy in the background. PHOTO: WHYTE MUSEUM OF THE CANADIAN ROCKIES, GEORGE NOBLE FONDS (V469/2594).

LEFT Edward's cabin on the acreage where he and Martha lived from 1915 to 1960. PHOTO: WHYTE MUSEUM OF THE CANADIAN ROCKIES, EDWARD FEUZ FONDS (DETAIL OF V200/I/A/II/ PA-669).

OPPOSITE Edward leading Georgia Engelhard and Tony (Eaton) Cromwell on a 1941 first ascent of a tower on Mount Murchison. PHOTO: EATON CROMWELL; WHYTE MUSEUM OF THE CANADIAN ROCKIES, EDWARD FEUZ FONDS (V200/I/A/II/PA-439).

OPPOSITE ABOVE The five guides with their partners sitting on the steps of Guide House in 1929. Top row: Walter Feuz, Ernst Feuz, Rudolf Aemmer and Christian Häsler. Bottom row: Elise Feuz, Rosa Häsler, Johanna Feuz (with two children, Ron and Syd), an unidentified friend and Martha and Edward Feuz. PHOTO: HANS LÜSCHER; STEPHEN COLLECTION.

OPPOSITE BELOW Rudolf and Edward at their retirement party at Guide House in 1949, with their hosts. PHOTO: WHYTE MUSEUM OF THE CANADIAN ROCKIES, EDWARD FEUZ FONDS (V200/A/I/II/ PA-550).

ABOVE Edward and Martha at home in 1969. PHOTO: FRANK STEPHEN; STEPHEN COLLECTION.

OPPOSITE Edward and Martha's dog, Janet, at Lake Louise in winter. PHOTO: EDWARD FEUZ; STEPHEN COLLECTION.

ABOVE A CPR 4-6-4 Royal Hudson steaming through the mountains. PHOTO: WHYTE MUSEUM OF THE CANADIAN ROCKIES, NICHOLAS MORANT FONDS (V500/I/C1/6/PA-28).

LEFT Edward and Rudolf (l–r) waiting for the train at Lake Louise. PHOTO: WHYTE MUSEUM OF THE CANADIAN ROCKIES, EDWARD FEUZ FONDS (V200/I/A/II/PA-483).

OPPOSITE Edward with professors Charles Fay and Joseph Hickson in August 1930, at the first hut built by the Alpine Club of Canada. The hut was named for Fay. PHOTO: WHYTE MUSEUM OF THE CANADIAN ROCKIES, EDWARD FEUZ FONDS (V200/I/A/II/PA-534).

ABOVE Pack horses at the large crevasse with its custom-made ladder, built to aid in the transport of construction materials for Abbot Pass Hut. PHOTO: EDWARD FEUZ; WHYTE MUSEUM OF THE CANADIAN ROCKIES, EDWARD FEUZ FONDS (V200/I/A/II/PA-72A).

BELOW The new Swiss-style alpine climbing hut at Abbot Pass, built in 1922. PHOTO: WHYTE MUSEUM OF THE CANADIAN ROCKIES, EDWARD FEUZ FONDS (V200/I/A/II/PA-81B).

ABOVE A summit photo of Fred Field, Edward, W.O. Field and Joseph Biner on their 1924 marathon tour of the South Twin, a first ascent, and of the North Twin, a second ascent. PHOTO: WHYTE MUSEUM OF THE CANADIAN ROCKIES, EDWARD FEUZ FONDS (V200/I/A/II/PA-244).

BELOW "Rucksack Pass" with (clockwise) Snowpatch, Pigeon and Howser (south tower) spires, along with the ridge of Bugaboo Spire. PHOTO: EDWARD FEUZ; STEPHEN COLLECTION.

OPPOSITE Edward in his hobnail boots making his way down a rock band on Mount Forbes. PHOTO: WHYTE MUSEUM OF THE CANADIAN ROCKIES, EDWARD FEUZ FONDS (V200/I/A/I/PA-348).

ABOVE Edward (top) belaying Georgia Engelhard on Mount Marpole in 1941. PHOTO: EATON CROMWELL; WHYTE MUSEUM OF THE CANADIAN ROCKIES, EDWARD FEUZ FONDS (DETAIL OF V200/I/A/II/PA-443).

OPPOSITE Edward at Lake Agnes with the Devils Thumb in the background. PHOTO: WHYTE MUSEUM OF CANADIAN ROCKIES, EDWARD FEUZ FONDS (V200/I/A/II/PA-523).

ABOVE Edward in 1906 with Mr. Wabsaw and Jean Parker, one of the most able women climbers in the early years of Edward's career. PHOTO: WHYTE MUSEUM OF CANADIAN ROCKIES, EDWARD FEUZ FONDS (DETAIL OF V200/I/A/II/PA-17).

OPPOSITE Taking in the view from Pinnacle Peak. Mount Fay is in the background. PHOTO: EDWARD FEUZ, STEPHEN COLLECTION.

OPPOSITE Edward with Jimmy the jacket thief. PHOTO: PAT STEPHEN; STEPHEN COLLECTION.

ABOVE On a backpacking trip. Left to right: Cindy, the author, Edward and Mike. PHOTO: PAT STEPHEN; STEPHEN COLLECTION.

BELOW Last-minute packing at Edward's house with Cindy, Mike, Edward and Frank. PHOTO: STEPHEN COLLECTION.

OPPOSITE ABOVE On the way to Abbot Pass in 1973. Left to right: Pat, Cindy, Mike and Edward. PHOTO: STEPHEN COLLECTION.

OPPOSITE BELOW Edward guiding the author on the Devils Thumb. PHOTO: STEPHEN COLLECTION.

ABOVE Cindy, Edward and Donna at Kain Hut in the Bugaboos in 1976. PHOTO: PAT STEPHEN, STEPHEN COLLECTION.

OPPOSITE Pat and Edward on Opabin Glacier, en route to Lake O'Hara from Moraine Lake in 1974. PHOTO: MIKE STEPHEN; STEPHEN COLLECTION.

ABOVE The author and Edward at Asulkan Glacier in 1977, on a three-day trip to see Mount Dawson. PHOTO: FRANK STEPHEN; STEPHEN COLLECTION.

Portrait of Edward Feuz Jr. PHOTO: NICHOLAS MORANT; BY PERMISSION OF ACHF/EXPORAIL, CANADIAN PACIFIC RAILWAY COMPANY FONDS (M505).

CHAPTER 7

READING THE SIGNS

In the days before air travel, guides were brought all the way from Europe at considerable expense to ensure that clients would survive to tell their tales of adventure in the Canadian Alps. The ultimate goal in guiding was to minimize risk while achieving the goal of reaching the summit if feasible, recognizing that there are many factors that are completely uncontrollable when dealing with nature. There are inherent risks when venturing into the mountains, and avoiding mishap is not always possible. Still, the watchword for guiding was, and still is, safety.

Knowledge, experience and good judgment are at the core of the guide's expertise. Although perfectly accurate assessment of given circumstances is not realistic, the guide needed to have a good ability to recognize and read – or interpret – the signs around him. Factors such as conditions on or near the mountain, the weather, the time required to reach the goal, and many other variables needed to be taken into consideration. Appropriate decisions based on Edward's reading of these data increased the probability of a successful and felicitous outing for the guest. For example, he might conclude that a rock wall on the route he has chosen is a "no-go" for the specific client he is guiding with the equipment and resources available to him on that particular day. The wall might be too difficult for the client, or too dangerous with only one guide. He might decide he will need a second rope or lighter shoes. Any number of things might lead him to conclude that climbing the wall is a bad idea. Having come to this conclusion, he would then have further decisions to make, such as whether or not he should try to find an alternative route on the mountain.

It can be difficult and disappointing to acknowledge that it is time to turn around on a mountain, especially when the summit is in sight. But sometimes this was what needed to be done when the risk of continuing was calculated to be too great. In such a philosophy, there is a thin line between dogged determination – what may at times be perceived as bravery – and foolishness. Blundering to the top of a mountain in dangerously poor conditions, when ill-equipped, with inadequate experience or with a deficient skill set, meant to Edward and his generation that you just got lucky. Maybe such an ascent was something to admit sheepishly – we all make mistakes – but it certainly was nothing to brag about. The novice who does not experience even fleeting feelings of fear in precipitous places is probably in over their head in more than the literal sense. In other words, the novice may not even have the ability to know what they have gotten themselves into, as they are oblivious to the hazards. Ignorance *is* bliss, but it also exacts a cost, whereas fear, an innate signalling system, is useful. It serves to get our attention so that we scan our environment for threats, identify them, ask rational questions of ourselves and make the best behavioural responses we can.

In Edward's day there was nothing glamorous or heroic about dying on a mountain. The goal was not to be a valiant martyr to the elements but rather to live to climb another day and another one after that. As a middle-aged guide was once heard to say, "I want to be doing this when I'm old." Adherence to this philosophy does not mean Edward backed off mountains easily. He was stubborn, did not like retreating unless absolutely necessary, and was adept at coaxing people to proceed beyond what they thought their limitations were. An ascent with a tricky section was an incentive for him, not a deterrent.

According to Howard Palmer, who climbed in and explored the mountains prior to 1920, existing maps were only vague sketches. This situation did not change until after the Boundary Commission in 1919, and it would be many years more before maps were produced and made available.[92]

Thus, the guides obtained data for navigational decision-making based on a combination of rough maps or notes (if others had gone before them), observation, and experience with terrain features similar to those they were assessing. Observation meant going to the mountain to reconnoitre. Edward often said, "I took a look at it with the [field] glasses." With observation based on experience and knowledge, one can get the lay of the land. Then one can identify the best way to go and assess difficulties and challenges which might be likely along the way, including whether or not the objective is too difficult for the client. Of course, there is no substitute for actually encountering the terrain.

Outfitted in a "slicker" (so nice to have more sophisticated gear now such as lightweight GORE-TEX rain pants), there are always civilized trails one can hike on even in rough weather. Climbing is a different matter. Wet rock is slippery and therefore dangerous. The threat of an electrical storm when one is exposed above the treeline is also cause for considerable concern. "If you feel buzzing, throw your ice axe away," warned Edward. Since he'd been knocked down himself by lightning on Mount Assiniboine, it was advice based on first-hand experience. Weather forecasting – for all its inaccuracies – does become a skill of the mountain guide on which calculated risks are taken.

A bonfire shot red and orange sparks into the night sky as a dancer in an eerie wooden mask, channelling his ancient Helvetian heritage, beseeched the spirits of nature for snow. Within a few days of the invocation it would snow, much to the glee of those who enjoy sliding on the stuff. The snow-inducing dancer was the fun-loving Bruno Engler, Swiss guide, whose ancestors were unlikely to have asked the spirits for snow.

Unlike Bruno, Edward never claimed to have induced snowfall, and he probably was not particularly interested in doing so, but he always seemed to be correct about whether it would rain or be a fine dry day. Both Bruno's ability to "induce" snow and the guides' more mundane facility for weather forecasting were contingent on a common instrument found hanging on the walls of Swiss homes – the barometer.* Now, we can wear them on our wrists.

Forecasting the weather; assessing snow and ice conditions; scanning the terrain for the best route; being prepared for unpleasant possibilities such as needing to spend a chilly and uncomfortable night on the mountain – all of these pall compared to reading "people" signs. The point of all this guiding activity is to get another human being, with their specific mental and physical strengths, weaknesses and eccentricities, to the top of a mountain.

Thinking of himself as a part of nature, and knowing that animals do not tend to spend their lives developing scary new methods of ambushing humans, Edward offered sensible advice. "Don't worry about the animals; it's the *people* you have to watch out for." Humans, he believed, with their predilection for impulsive and irrational behaviour, are far less predictable than animals and should be watched with a wary eye.

Thorington wrote about an incident which offers a case in point:

> An outfitter, waking suddenly in the night at the scratching of a small animal at the tent door, and with dreams of a grizzly still confusing him, fired his gun point-blank. The porcupine seems to have escaped unscathed, but a gaping hole was blown in the side of the folding boat [cached outside the tent].[93]

* Weather is an obsession in extreme climates. Martha Feuz kept weather notes recording the temperature daily, across decades.

To teenage girls Edward added a coda to his advice about people: "Don't hook up with boys, they do foolish things." Sage advice, from someone who ought to know.

Edward had an excellent ability to read "people signs." He watched people interact and was good at noticing non-verbal cues. Bruno Engler, the aforementioned snow dancer, was an expert skier and skilled professional photographer. A younger-generation Swiss guide, born in Lugano in 1915, he had come to Canada in 1939 and was employed, for a time by the CPR, under Edward. As a young guide, he may have had some conflicts between his identity as photographer and his guiding responsibilities. Edward would certainly have understood a passion for photography and the many opportunities which would arise to engage this interest while guiding. Nevertheless, these agendas do not always mix well. Bruno, quoting the advice Edward had given him on this topic said, "When you are on the mountain you have to always be alert. You always have to look for the dangers, and every move you have to estimate. Don't say anything, but you always have to be looking at your guests."[94]

As children, we were led by Edward to a viewpoint overlooking the steep walls of a canyon, with the express purpose – although we did not know it at the time – of assessing how we would react to heights, just as we were evaluated in other settings as to balance, strength and endurance. Joseph Hickson, despite his impressive climbing résumé, had one specific weakness. He simply could not cross moving water. On one occasion, Edward used his ice axe to hook the professor by his suspenders and fish him out of the torrent. This was not very dignified from the point of view of the faux fish himself, but it was better than drowning. Even cutting down excessively large trees to use as makeshift bridges did not ameliorate the problem. And no matter what tricks Edward used to inspire him to avoid looking down, Hickson could not train himself to resist this impulse. As soon as he glanced downward, in he went. Understandably very embarrassed by this weakness, Hickson recounted one attempt to cross water which succeeded. Again trees were felled to make "a sort of bridge that I always detest crossing over swiftly running water." He goes on to explain the reason for his success: "Fortunately, it was still dark when we crossed the stream, so I could not see clearly what was underneath."[95]

In a similar fashion to the assessments Edward made of our skills, the guides would avoid taking a total stranger, with their uncharted propensities, on a serious or committed climb, until they passed more minor tests such as a steep walk on talus or an ascent of the Devils Thumb or similar mountain. The Devils Thumb was perfect as a "test mountain." It is close to the Chateau and involves a hike and some scrambling. If one wishes, some climbing with an intense drop-off can be accomplished before reaching the summit, with its lovely view. The descent involves negotiating steep and loose terrain. Thus in one reasonably easy day a whole host of client skills could be assessed while still giving guests a pleasant time in the outdoors.

The luxury of test climbs was possible because guests often stayed at the Chateau for extended periods of time – sometimes months – so there was usually plenty of opportunity for multiple excursions. George Engelhard, a prominent New York lawyer, was one guest with sufficient resources to spend a whole summer with his family at Chateau Lake Louise. His wife, Agnes Stieglitz Engelhard, was the sister of Alfred Stieglitz, a renowned New York photographer who was a tireless advocate for the acceptance of photography as fine art. He was also an art impresario who was instrumental in introducing talents such as Pablo Picasso to American audiences.[96] His partner was one of the many American artists he promoted, Georgia O'Keeffe. George and Agnes Engelhard's daughter, Georgia, showed an early predilection for art. She had regular correspondence with her uncle Alfred and was given an exhibition at his famous 291 gallery when she was only 10 years old. Called "Georgia Minor," she painted at her aunt's side and developed a style which to some extent mirrored the famous artist's.[97]

As a young woman on holiday with her family at the Chateau, Georgia was initially more interested in dining and dancing than climbing, as she had a tremendous fear of heights. With repeated exposure, she quickly conquered this fear. Thereafter she became an avid mountaineer (and skilled photographer), spending a considerable part of her life climbing in Canada and making numerous first ascents. She also climbed in Switzerland and later lived there, selling her mountain photography and stories to magazines. Sadly, her mountaineering days were ended later in life when a London taxicab ran over her foot.*

Edward once took Martha to Abbot Pass Hut, and although she did well from a technical perspective, she was terrified the whole way, and unlike Georgia, never developed into a mountaineer. Martha loved being amongst the mountains – some of her fondest memories were having school days alfresco in the alp-lands – she just did not like being up on the mountains themselves. And so it is with human preferences.

For some guests, a guided hike would be thrill enough to last a lifetime. With someone who may have been apprehensive about heights, their own abilities and scary narrow trails (or no trails), the trick, Edward believed, is to avoid revealing too much information. Obfuscate if necessary, keep people moving (slowly and at a constant pace), distracted and under the impression that all they have to do is follow along. Many a neophyte discovered pleasure and pride in the "sudden" realization that they had attained the summit of a pass or hill which just a few hours earlier they would have deemed an improbable, if not impossible, goal.

Ethel Johns** described this "following along" with what seems to have been her typical sense of humour. Responding to the query of how she liked the view on her climb, she wrote:

* Georgia Engelhard Cromwell was born in 1906 in New York City. She died in 1986, at Interlaken, Switzerland.

** Ethel Johns (1879–1968) was a nurse, writer and early Alpine Club of Canada member.

As a matter of fact all I saw on the way up [Mount] Huber was Edouard's boots. They pervaded the whole landscape and rose and fell with the regularity of clockwork. Occasionally, *very* occasionally, these boots were near enough to be studied in detail, but more often I had to content myself with mere impressionistic glimpses of them disappearing upwards, ever upwards.[98]

On the same trip, Johns had been instructed by Edward to stick her feet in the snow and quit walking like a chicken. Admonishment that in retrospect is humorous can help sometimes. Lillian Gest, a Philadelphian with a long connection to the mountains, was once leading an easy climb at Lake O'Hara when a young woman in her party suddenly became hysterical, terrified she would fall. Gest dealt with it by remarking drily, "My dear, you couldn't *throw* yourself off that ledge." Startled into a more rational perspective on her situation, the woman finished the climb.[99]

Sometimes the guide needs stubborn insistence in dealing with hesitant guests. Ms. Lulu Grau of Honolulu, writing of a climb in 1905 up Avalanche Peak in the Selkirks, related:

We encountered again some difficulty in crossing the Bergschrund on our way down, but Eduard proved himself master of the situation and had no pity on me when I declared myself unable to cross the Schrund where he wanted me to. I simply had to do it and accomplished the seemingly impossible feat quite easily after all."[100]

An apprehensive Howard Palmer had required more than verbal insistence when his party reached a steep and exposed section near the summit of Mount Sir Sandford. The rock was covered with ice and there was a nasty-looking cornice above them. Palmer did not think they should go on, stating in his account of the climb, "The whole situation looked almost prohibitively dangerous, for there were no real holds or anchorages whatever..."[101] Speaking only in Swiss, the guides ignored his concerns and moved into action. Edward, while distracting Palmer, began belaying, as Rudolf chopped about fifteen steps in the ice. The clients sat on a rocky knob below, taking photos. Palmer commented, "We held our breath as we watched him, for, to all intents and purposes, he was on the brink of eternity."[102] When it became time to move, Palmer, who was resisting doing so, received "a little shove" from Edward. Struggling to regain his feet and already in motion, Palmer was able to continue on his own when seconds earlier, thinking it was too dangerous, he had refused to move.

Edward did not have as much success on Mount Sir Donald with the German man who proudly declared that he had climbed the Matterhorn. The resultant fiasco was a clear justification for test climbs. Although skeptical about the man's suitability for the climb, Edward ultimately agreed to guide him up. On a second rope, Chris Häsler was leading another guest. Sadly, as soon as Edward's client began climbing, it became evident that he was not very experienced. Nevertheless, Edward managed to safely lead the man up the mountain, to a point only a hundred feet (about thirty metres) from the destination. It was there that the man stopped climbing, for some inexplicable reason, and refused to go any farther. He could not be budged, despite Edward jerking the rope and resorting to cajoling and pleading – in short, using all the reasonable techniques at his disposal. Having no other choice, Edward waited where they were on the mountain with his guest, while Chris and his client finished the climb. Then came the descent.

As Edward told it, "On the way down my 'Matterhorn man' got panicky on the vertical rock and wouldn't move. I had to get down below him and take his feet in my hands and put them on each foothold." The man's "paralysis" was obviously sheer terror, and equally obviously it created a dangerous situation on the mountain. The effort on Edward's part would have been unbelievably difficult, but he had to get the man down somehow. As fate would have it, Matterhorn man was then hit a glancing blow on the head by a falling rock and knocked unconscious. As the now oblivious guest swung through the air, Edward, with the greatest of difficulty, managed to hang onto the rock and thus not be pulled off the mountain himself. "When he [the client] came to," said Edward, "the first thing he said was he had never climbed the Matterhorn. Fortunately, his bump on the head did not prove to be serious beyond making him honest"[103]

Unlike Matterhorn man, Alice Newell learned to cope with her fear rationally and did not need a rockfall-induced attitude adjustment. Writing in Edward's *Führer-Buch* in 1941 she said, "Due to his excellent guidance and teaching, a wonderful new door in life has been opened to me." What she meant was that Edward had helped her overcome her fear of heights. She added, charmingly, that he did this "by impressing upon me one of life's most essential values. Concentrate on what lies before you, and don't give in to fear."[104]

In a scenario similar to Matterhorn man, Bruno Engler tells the story of "the dandy," which is set in the same time period when Alice Newell was earning her stripes as a real mountaineer.

Edward took an instant dislike to the pale fellow who showed up at Lake Louise all dressed up in light-coloured trousers, a blazer and white shoes. Gesturing toward Mount Victoria, he asked Edward if he had ever climbed the mountain. Wrong question. Just before stomping off to Guide House, Edward, springing to his feet, removed the pipe from his mouth and barked, "I've climbed that mountain more times than you have hairs on your head."

Meanwhile, through a gambit aimed at dissuading the man from ambitions on the mountain by telling him how expensive it would be, Bruno instead entangled Edward in the task of taking the man up the mountain. Hearing from Bruno that the man had bragged about having climbed in the Alps "so this will be nothing," Edward decided to teach him a lesson.

After a stroll to the Plain of Six Glaciers teahouse and a snack, the trio descended the steep slope over loose rocks on their way to the glacier. By this point the fellow had already fallen on his backside – several times. It was not a good omen. But onto the glacier they went, roped up by then, Edward in front and Bruno in the rear. Gazing into the blue abyss at the edge of big crevasse, the dandy balked; he was even too scared to brag. Coaxing convinced him to cross the snow bridge. After this success, Edward announced, "Now we will show you what a mountain is all about." Off they went up the steeper section of the glacier to the hut. The next morning, they arose to a dense fog. "Good," murmured the client, "we'll have to go back." Edward was ready for this response. Smiling, he answered: "Nothing doing. We'll start for the top very soon. The sun will be shinning on the summit ridge. This is just a local inversion. When the sun comes up, it will soon melt away."

After roping up in the hut, which is what one does on this climb, they set off in a fog so thick that Bruno could not even see Edward above him. He did not worry, though. As he put it, "Edward could find that route blindfolded." Suddenly a shout was heard from Edward, announcing he had reached the ridge, which was, as he had predicted, in full sunlight. Thinking he had arrived at the summit, the client began to relax, but that was shortlived. "No," responded the guides. "You see that long, narrow snow ridge? The summit is a kilometre across that ridge." The way forward looked particularly intimidating on that day early in the climbing season, as there was still a lot of snow. "To a novice," Bruno said, "it must have looked like a knife-edge across the void." And when the man protested with, "I'm happy right here," Bruno jumped right in and said: "Nothing doing. You paid to go to the top and this is not the top." A few epithets in Swiss could be heard as the guides prepared to move on toward the summit, with the reluctant guest in tow.

Arriving at a portion of the ridge called the "sickle," they proceeded cautiously, as Edward needed to cut some steps. He advised Bruno to walk close to the man and not let him straddle the ridge. Enthusiastically complying with these instructions, Bruno held on to the man by the "scruff of his neck and seat of his pants." Farther along, the snow was so thick with cornices (snow which overhangs from the rock or snow without any support and is therefore very dangerous) that Edward and Bruno released a few of them with their ice axes, causing a huge avalanche down the precipitous wall. Likely startled by the rumbling of falling snow, the client chose this moment to fall through another cornice, in other words to step into mere air. Being on a short rope he did not go far, but Bruno decided it was time for a stern lecture: "Watch where Edward is going. Follow his footprints. Don't walk like a drunken sailor on a New York City street!"

Finally reaching the summit, the dandy, too traumatized to enjoy the view or even eat asked, weakly, if they were going back the same way. Edward, softening, reassured him. "Don't worry. We'll get you down safe and sound." So, with Edward pulling on the rope from the front and Bruno helping from behind, they managed to arrive back at the hut. But apparently the client was a truly compulsive braggart, because he started in again as soon as he felt safe. Edward, interrupting him with some reality testing, said, "Don't get too cocky. We still have to go down the Death Trap. I'd rather be on that [summit] ridge than in that hole."

On the way down the glaciated pass, the dandy, whether dim-witted, narcissistic or just too terrified to think, failed to adhere to Bruno's earlier dictate to follow in Edward's steps and, with a mighty scream, fell into a crevasse. Sighing, Edward and Bruno hauled him up and on they all went until, mercifully for all concerned, the climb was over. Then the dandy, much to their surprise, thanked the guides in terse German. Realizing the man might have understood some of the ongoing Swiss commentary which accompanied the trip, Bruno exclaimed, "No wonder we didn't get a tip!"

"It doesn't matter," Edward answered. "We taught him not to lie and brag about the mountains."[105]

Those who climbed with Edward (and with the Swiss guides in general) ranged in skill from the extremely competent to individuals who, like the dandy, might have been hauled like sacks of laundry. However, even relatively competent climbers refer to having been assisted by "several short jerks" of the rope on a particularly devilish bit. Although it may be gratifying to think we could be "hauled" up through a tough spot if need be, most of us today would find being given short jerks while we are climbing quite annoying. To say that all the guides' clients were hauled is a gross over-generalization and simply not true. Edward acknowledged that many people he guided climbed well. Significant numbers of those were women, who had a greater tendency to take direction and were "neater with their feet." He felt Jean

Parker, daughter of the Winnipeg journalist Elizabeth Parker, was one of the best women he had climbed with in his early years in Canada.[106]

Clients' relationships with guides were both positive and ambivalent. The divergence in their respective perceptions of events can be quite amusing if one knows (or can intuit from experience) the guide's perspective. The accounts of Matterhorn man and the dandy are clearly from the perspective of the guides – Edward and Bruno. It would be a fairly safe bet that their clients' post-climb stories were at least sprinkled with boasts and riddled with omissions.

Sometimes clients can be caught out in print. Joseph Hickson, describing the first ascent of Pinnacle, seems quite forthright: "For a few minutes I had almost regretted that I had come..." Sitting straddled on a rocky crest while waiting for Edward to find the way forward, he described "a sheer drop on either side of probably 2,000 feet" and, on the pitch Edward was leading, an absence of handholds. Although Hickson did manage to continue the climb, handholds or not, he described other conditions on the mountain as engendering "considerable tension" and the necessity of a "keen outlook [being] constantly demanded to meet an emergency which was not at all improbable"[107] From these dramatic words: "sheer drop," "no handholds," "considerable tension," "regret" and a possible "emergency" one can infer that the climber was more than a wee bit nervous, conscious of danger and perceiving himself to be in a difficult situation.

But years later, writing with more bravado, Hickson

said, "Pinnacle Mountain is still an interesting climb and affords capital exercise for training purposes."[108] How unbecoming of him to seek to diminish such a nice little peak, one which did not succumb to his advances so easily and which, Edward would add, scared the pants off him.

In the old climbing guidebooks, the clients who made first ascents with guides were listed first, followed by the names of the guide (or guides) in italics, even though it was the latter who led, chose the routes, were charged with ensuring the person got up and down the mountain safely, and stood on top first. Edward took his job seriously. "When you have people behind you and you are responsible for them, you have to look after them."[109] He viewed guiding as a vocation, something he was trained to do, and he was rightfully proud of his skills. And yet there is clearly an ambivalent attitude on the part of some clients. To use the aforementioned client/author as an example (even though he was not at all singular), Hickson described Pinnacle as having "succumbed two years later to [his] efforts, aided by the two Swiss guides E. Feuz Jr. and Rudolf Aemmer...."[110] If one remembers how petrified Hickson was while he waited for Edward not only to find the way but also to climb it first and then belay him, it is easy to see from the guide's point of view that the client would be blatantly overstating his own role and minimizing that of the guide.*

* Also keep in mind there was little protection for the guide, or leader, in the days before placing "hardware" made leading considerably safer.

To his credit, Hickson was an ardent mountaineer who Edward said had more stamina than any other client he had climbed with, despite having an unsteady gait due to an old injury. But seriously, "aided" by the guides? Well, the client could brag all he wanted, but the guides knew the truth.

I always knew Edward to be generous in his praise of others and to give credit where it was warranted, as he did when praising Hickson's stamina. When asked what he thought of Conrad Kain, the Austrian mountain guide, Edward said Kain was a very good rock climber and a nice fellow, and he wished he could have hired him. He also spoke with some respect about guests he had guided who he felt were deserving of such. However, in the mountains even those with high status were just human beings with foibles, like all of us. If some needed a firm hand, to be instructed to quit walking like a chicken, or even required a shove, this is what they received from Edward.

Admittedly there were some from the "upper classes" whom he simply disliked because they were annoyingly authoritarian or overtly disrespectful. Having heard stories of the disdainful behaviour and arrogance some people displayed by virtue of privilege, it was no wonder that not all were cherished.

There was one particularly troublesome fellow who was very well known and, from what I perceive in reading about him, quite taken with himself. At times he was a hazard to himself and others, habitually refused to be roped up and repeatedly tried to usurp Edward's authority; generally, he was a nuisance to deal with. Once, coming down a mountain, with four people behind him under his care, including the oppositional one, Edward needed to cut some steps on an icy section. "All at once [Edward] heard a little noise and here was [the arrogant client] sliding down the ice patch on his pants. If it hadn't been for me [Edward having nabbed him just in time], he'd have slid down a thousand-foot cliff."[111]

Although he would not have relayed this story earlier in his career, except perhaps in Swiss or in confidence, later in life this was a way of taking such a person "down a peg." For Edward, the most important purpose in telling such a story was not to boast but to convey some of the trials he faced in doing his job – in this example, the serious scenario resulting from the actions of an unco-operative client who happened to be of "high status."

Employed by the class-conscious CPR, Edward was always aware of his own status as a "working man," albeit at the top of the working-man totem pole. The class system was glaringly apparent sometimes. In the journal of the Alpine Club of Canada, a report read: "The two Swiss guides, Edouard Feuz and Gottfried Feuz, of Interlaken, who were at the Yoho Camp, were placed at the disposal of the Club by the courtesy of Mr. Hayter Reed, Manager-in-Chief of the C.P.R. hotels, for the week of the meet."[112] The language is odd to our ears nowadays, sounding as if the writer is commending Mr. Reed for generously loaning out a vehicle or a piece of equipment.

Sir Winston S. Churchill, as a boy in his first term at Harrow, related:

The school possessed the biggest swimming-bath I had ever seen... Naturally it was a good joke to come up behind some naked friend, or even enemy, and push him in... One day when I had been no more than a month in the school, I saw a boy standing in a meditative posture wrapped in a towel on the very brink... Coming stealthily behind, I pushed him in, holding on to his towel out of humanity, so that it should not get wet... Swift as the wind my pursuer overtook me, seized me in a ferocious grip and hurled me into the deepest part of the pool. I soon scrambled out on the other side, and found myself surrounded by an agitated crowd of younger boys. "You're in for it," they said. "Do you know what you've done? It's Amery; he's in the Sixth Form. He is the head of his House; he is champion at gym; he has got his football colours"... I was convulsed not only with terror but with the guilt of sacrilege. How could I tell his rank when he was in a bath-towel and so small?[113]

Sir Winston goes on to say: "I have been fortunate to see a good deal more of him, in times when three years' difference in age is not so important as it is at school. We were afterwards to be Cabinet colleagues for a good many years."[114]

Edward said about him, "Amery was a lovely person, *a small little man* [my emphasis], didn't talk very much, very nice to travel with. We were out a whole month together."[115]

It seems Amery kept his class attitudes to himself, at least in the presence of Edward, who would have been stunned to know that it was this "lovely person" who had had taken it upon himself to settle the Swiss guides in Canada. It apparently did not occur to him to consider whether this was what the guides would have wanted. The extent of his erstwhile prejudice, and what certainly seems to have been arrogance, is apparent from a note he wrote as a younger man in the Glacier House scrapbook in 1905. In it, he recommended that the guides be paid the way they are in Switzerland and commented, for all to read, "At present there is no real inducement to the guide to choose the good climbs, or indeed to climb at all, & there are so many competing for them, that they tend to become both lazy & unduly filled with a sense of their own importance." Breathtaking.

Whether Amery had matured by the time Edward met him or at least outgrown some of his now outrageous but in earlier times not unusual class prejudices, we can assume by Edward's assessment of him that he was at least overtly civil. He also appears to have been rather stubborn and not exactly comprehending of the wilderness experience he was immersed in. One of the peaks they were to climb in 1929 was Mount Amery. Of course, it was a first ascent.

Edward recounted that they began travelling along the Alexandra River at 3:00 a.m. in threatening weather, but Edward figured they could always turn around in the trees if the weather remained poor. As they emerged above the treeline, the weather was still not good and

Edward said, "Well, colonel, it doesn't look to be a very nice day. I think we should go back. We should have a nice day going on there on the first ascent. You can't see very well and it's not much pleasure."

Amery in a polite and gentle way responded, "Yes, but we don't turn around in Switzerland when we climb the mountains, do we?"

Edward then needed to explain to him that in Switzerland the situation was different because there were "signs" as to how one should proceed. He added, "I've never been up this mountain before. I've got to find it [the way] first. It's a different thing [than in Switzerland], but if you insist to go, I can stand as much as you, colonel. So say yes or no."

On they went. And the weather became so bad that they had to crawl on their hands and knees. Edward commented that he only had ten or fifteen feet of visibility; by this time, the snow that had been falling was sticking to their eyelashes. They did make it to the summit, and while Edward made a stone man [cairn] Amery was lying prone out of the storm "to rest his face!"

The descent was slow because in addition to poor visibility, the handholds were wet and slippery and they needed to be extra careful. By the time they reached the trees it was pitch black. Edward lit a candle in a lantern and walked behind, so the colonel could see where to go. Edward remarked, "He was so tired, the poor chap, that he could hardly lift his feet anymore." Observing this, he suggested they should build a nice fire for warmth and stop for the night, figuring it would take them the remainder of the night to walk "home" (that is, to their camp).

"Oh no, we don't do that in Switzerland. We go right down to the hut," was the response. Edward patiently explained that there were *trails* in Switzerland which one could easily follow at night. And, they were not descending to the safety and comfort of a hut as they would have been in Europe.

The colonel remained obdurate, despite his obvious fatigue, and on they went. That is, they went on for only another quarter of an hour, when Amery suddenly announced that Edward's idea of stopping for the night was a splendid one. So Edward found a stream he had heard a few minutes away and there they stopped. He built a fire, prepared tea and made a bough bed for Amery. Within five minutes of drinking his tea, Amery was snoring and had to be awakened to eat dinner.

The next morning, when Amery expressed a desire to take a bath, Edward obliged. He dug a hole (typically not any easy thing to do in the Rocky Mountains), lined it with a canvas tarp and filled it with hot water.

Two days later Amery was worried they had not actually reached the summit in the storm. To resolve the issue Edward took him up a relatively easy neighbouring peak – Mount Saskatchewan, which is over 11,000 feet high. It was a lovely day, and reaching the top he sat Amery on the edge with field glasses and directed him to look right across at his mountain, Mount Amery. "He took the glass and smiled and said, 'You're right, Edward. It's right on the very top.'"

Near the end of their month-long trip together, they had another day with beautiful weather, and of course Edward thought they should climb a little peak, which they did. He described the way they finished their climb this way: "I stepped back near the summit and said, 'Okay, colonel, I think this is a first ascent; you may as well be the first. You go ahead.'"

Amery responded, "What do you mean? You're the guide, Edward." Edward continued, "Never mind that, you be the guide for a change. You be the first to put a foot on the mountain. That's a nice little peak."

Edward said Amery "smiled and went ahead and was he ever happy."[116] When he arrived home to his post as colonial secretary in the British government, Amery wrote a note to CPR Hotels:

> I should like to send just a line to say how thoroughly satisfied I was with the services of Edward Feuz during the month we were climbing together this summer. He is a most competent and prudent guide and has got a great eye for finding the right way up the mountain as well as the technical skill for actually seeing through the business. He is also a very pleasant and helpful companion both climbing and on the trail.[117]

Perhaps the "helpfulness" was a reference to the guide having built him a custom bathtub! Whether Amery viewed Edward as a servant (if so, ironically a servant he felt confident entrusting with his very life and limb) Edward certainly did not see himself in this light.

For the most part, strong bonds of friendship were formed between client and guide despite class attitudes. And people clamoured for Edward's attention. This is easy to understand, as in addition to being known as a superior guide with exacting standards for himself, he was easy to like and eager to share his enthusiasm for mountains.

Edward's perspective on guide/client relationships was that the "hardship" of climbing was conducive to developing deep personal connections. Most remarks about him by clients were glowing and respectful. Alice Newell, whom Edward helped to overcome her fear of heights, wrote, "Not only has he great skill and judgment as a mountaineer but his splendid comradeship has added so very much to the joy of my love of climbing and the mountains."[118]

Even Hickson wrote of Edward that his "intelligent and sympathetic enthusiasm, combined with a strong individualism, gives him a first place among the Rocky Mountain professionals..."[119] And in 1951 Bert Wiebrecht, a dentist from Milwaukee, Wisconsin, wrote this lovely tribute:

> It was 1934 that we first met at Assiniboine, and thru these many years you have taught me to love the mountains. Fortunate indeed is the man who has had the privilege of climbing with you, as I have, as no guide has greater ability, skill or judgment. But above all of this I cherish your friendship, your incomparable comradeship, thru which you have

instilled the peace and contentment that only the mountains can bring to the soul of a man.[120]

Reaching the summit was the portent of a pleasant and successful workday for Edward and a memorable achievement for a honeymoon couple he guided. The latter had climbed well and were justifiably pleased with their accomplishment. After the rewards of a rest and hearty luncheon, the little party readied themselves for the descent. Suddenly the woman, who had been fine moments before, began crying and screaming incoherently. Her new husband tried to calm her – alas without success – and her distress continued to escalate. They were a few thousand feet above level ground, surrounded by a rocky drop-off in all directions. There was no one in the vicinity who could help them. Their only viable option – meant in the most literal sense – was to climb down.

Edward knew the protocol for hysteria. Give the individual a firm slap on the face, he reminded himself. However, in this particular situation there was the complicating factor of the distraught husband. Surely he would object to the application of this particular remedy. What am I to do? Edward wondered. Suddenly the answer came to him and he acted. In the distracting atmosphere engendered by emotional chaos, Edward slowly manoeuvred the woman to the edge of the precipice. Holding her on a short rope, he bumped her sharply with his hip. Over the cliff she went, stopping with a sudden jerk. The husband, unaware of what had been happening, stood stunned as Edward carefully hauled the woman back up the cliff. After a few moments of consultation and assessment, it was determined that she was fine.

They climbed down the mountain as efficiently and cheerfully as they had ascended. It was as if nothing extraordinary at all had happened. Despite the emotional episode which ended in a "hip check," the client turned out to be what Edward would call a good sport.[121] It is not known whether the couple ever climbed again, but they certainly had a good story to tell about their first days together – even without the embarrassingly dramatic bits. Perhaps they regaled their grandchildren with the tale: "We climbed a mountain on our honeymoon!"

CHAPTER 8

SNAPSHOTS

It is [my] profound conviction that the near
presence of Feuz is a continual menace to the
yet untrodden peaks of the Canadian Alps.

— HOWARD PALMER, SECRETARY OF THE
AMERICAN ALPINE CLUB, 1915*

On our way up the beautifully graded Swiss switchback trail, the sun had become obscured by high, thin,
quickly moving grey clouds. Despite fingers too cool to
grip sandwiches comfortably and postures too hunched
to be relaxed, we still sat on the narrow rocky pass taking in the view. We had surveyed the scene from Sentinel
Pass before. Each of us, in our own separate way, knew it
well. Perhaps frequent exposure to beautiful views had
allowed us to absorb Edward's appreciative attitude, because sitting quietly in familiar mountain places had become an immersive experience for us as it had always
been for Edward. Nevertheless, random memories and
thoughts did intrude. Daydreams of climbing the peaks
we could see would suddenly be interrupted by mundane
yearnings for a milkshake we might drink later that day.

* *Führer-Buch*

Pat and Cindy certainly thought about snow patches they might glissade on as we made our way down. Mike had memories of a sleekly groomed but thin-looking "Lassie" he had met while the dog was starring in a movie being filmed in Larch Valley. Memories rushed toward Edward from every peak he could see. Despite the compelling tug these exerted, he always managed to be in the present too, maintaining the ability to experience afresh both the serenity and the excitement such vistas evoke.

Suddenly our reveries ended when Edward raised his head to the sky and in a very loud but beseeching voice said, "Come on, sun, give us a little!" And considerately, the sun obliged. No one was surprised that Edward, who at heart was a kind of animist, should bellow requests of the sun, or even that it should comply.

Sentinel Pass was named for the grand stone guardians of Paradise Valley. With its stunning alpine views, situated between Pinnacle Mountain and Mount Temple, this pass was a favourite of Edward's and one he liked to share with friends and clients. We saw it in all kinds of weather – with rain pelting down, snow swirling around us, and on days with bluebird skies.

I know that many a novice taking in the views of the peaks nestling the surreally blue Moraine Lake, and further distracted by a swath of larch trees, a wooden bridge over a peaceful stream and plentiful wildflowers lining the trail, would almost unknowingly find themselves atop this 2611-metre pass. There they would marvel that they had travelled on their own two feet to such a height in the company of no less than a famous Swiss guide.

The "tourist route" on Mount Temple, the highest peak in the Lake Louise area, begins on this pass. Ascending the southwest flank to the ridge, this is the easiest route to the 11,626-foot (3543-metre) summit, but it is not a hike as some people purport. There are cliff bands to contend with and significant objective hazards. Edward always warned us to stay well away from the climber's right, upon reaching the glacier near the summit. The reason for this – a cornice to make one's knees quake – is in full view when travelling from the opposite (northeast) ridge. At least one unfortunate person has dropped through this cornice, never to be seen again.

There are numerous other routes on this mountain, including several that ascend the dramatic north face (first climbed in the 1960s), but it was up the tourist route that the average client was guided, generally reaching the summit (from Moraine Lake) in seven and a half hours. Edward climbed this peak for the last time four months shy of his 81st birthday. He had wanted to do it the previous summer, but it had not been feasible that year. The following winter, he was singularly obsessed with achieving this goal, or as he put it, "it bothered me the whole winter."

Finally summer came and Edward found two agreeable companions – his friend Phyllis Hart and John Linn, the pianist at the Chateau Lake Louise – to accompany him. Their climb started from Larch Valley and began, Edward recalled, as a "half and half day, but as we went up the weather seemed to improve." Nevertheless, all the way Edward felt a sense of impending disappointment that he should likely "not get the view on top – because I wanted to see way up north, to see Mount Columbia, Forbes and all those big peaks I climbed years and years ago." His pessimism seemed justified, as fortune did not seem to be with him: "We got up to the top and we couldn't see a thing; we couldn't even take a picture. We stayed there an hour and nearly froze to death." Finally admitting there was no hope, he said, "Let's go home." Thus, after five hours of toiling, it seemed Edward had missed his last opportunity to see some of "his mountains."

They had retreated only a short way when "the clouds just disappeared around us and I could see my view!" In three and a half hours they were off the mountain, with Edward feeling tired (as anyone would) but gloriously happy. He did not keep records of each ascent he made in his long career, but he estimated he must have been up Temple fifty times.[122]

Later, when John Linn told the crowd at the evening concert about his 80-year-old guide's achievement, Edward was received with enthusiastic applause.

On the opposite side of Sentinel Pass from Mount Temple, Pinnacle Mountain had twice thwarted Edward before he and Rudolf along with their client Joseph Hickson finally made the first ascent on July 29, 1909. From Paradise Valley they had worked their way up friable rock to the col between Eiffel Peak and Pinnacle. From there they faced nearly vertical rock which they negotiated for several hours* before reaching a gully that was much easier ground.

In another 30 minutes they were sitting on the summit enjoying the warm sunshine (and some yodelling too, one hopes, as the echo from this summit is unparalleled) and taking in the views, which included the distinctive Mount Deltaform, the eighth of the ten peaks, called *Sarhnora* in Îyârhe (Stoney) Nakoda. About four weeks later the threesome would make what they thought was a second ascent of this mountain, but in fact would turn out to be a new route, at least in part, by virtue of the steep chimney they climbed, which the original party, led by the Kaufmanns, did not.[123]

At any rate, the descent of Pinnacle Mountain, which would complete a traverse of the peak, was even more exhilarating for Hickson than the ascent had been, as descending mountains often can be. In addition to the usual insecurities of moving downward on steep terrain, the ledge they were on ended abruptly, blocked by an odd rock feature. However, there was a small hole in the feature. Beyond the hole was a one-metre gap, below which, Hickson noted, there was a dramatically dark four-metre-deep pit. They would need to cross this gap (and thus the pit) to continue their progress down the mountain. Lying prone on the ledge, Hickson bridged the gap with his legs, then wriggled the rest of his body through the hole, pivoted sharply and gradually swung himself upright. He was assisted in making this seemingly awkward

---

* See the description in the previous chapter of how precarious Hickson felt their situation was on this ascent.

207 .

manoeuvre by Edward, who secured the rope for him on the other side of the gap. The climb, Hickson tells us, reached a grand finale with a 60-foot rappel. Although for Hickson it was a modified rappel, as the guides had tied a second rope around his waist. Given that Hickson admitted to "swinging once or twice like a bundle of goods" and feeling there might be a "permanent groove"[124] in the region of his midsection, a second rope was a wise precaution.

After the first ascent of Pinnacle, "permanent ropes" (the first in the Canadian Rockies) were affixed to the difficult pitch in order to assist guides in making the climb safer for clients. As Lillian Gest remarked, this was also an endeavour to make life easier on the guides, "who might be called on to climb such a peak four or five times in a two-week period"[125] for example, during an Alpine Club of Canada camp. For a client such as the ever keen Georgia Engelhard wanting to make a speedy ascent (in only three hours from Moraine Lake), it was one thing climbing hard pitches. For a guide who earned his living climbing day in and day out, it was a different matter. Whenever possible, they preferred to pace themselves.

Partway down the switchbacks from Sentinel Pass, a much older Edward than the man who had co-guided the first ascent of Pinnacle in 1909 reached a snow patch and, without a word of warning, literally jumped off the trail. Sitting on his short alpine hiking cane, he flew down the snow. We smiled and followed.

❃ ❃ ❃

On Mount Mitre he undoubtedly saved me from
being hurled down the face of the mountain
by a large stone I had unwittingly loosened.
My respect for Edward as a guide and my
liking for him as a man will always lead me to
give him a most sincere recommendation.

— JOSEPH WOOD JR., 1910, *FÜHRER-BUCH*

From the Plain of Six Glaciers teahouse (at Lake Louise)
one can see an attractive little peak called Mitre, named
for its resemblance to a bishop's headgear. At only 9,480
feet high (2890 metres), it is dwarfed by its neighbours
Mount Aberdeen at 10,340 feet (3152 metres) and Mount
Lefroy, 11,230 feet (3423 metres). The latter, close by, towers above it. The Mitre has a pleasing look about it – rugged and rocky with a tiny point for a top. One's eye is
drawn to it for its aesthetics and because of its compara-
tively diminutive size. Also, because it is not visible from
the shores of Lake Louise (being blocked by the taller
peaks), this pleasant surprise reveals itself only to those
willing to do a little work to see it.

In 1968 Edward decided he wanted to take us to Mitre
Pass – probably in part because of my enthusiasm for this
charming peak. We set off as we always did, early in the
morning, and began the walk around the lake toward the
teahouse. As we walked farther toward Victoria Glacier,
we could glimpse the Mitre just barely above the gentle
west shoulder of Mount Aberdeen. Once we were above

the treeline and Victoria loomed large ahead of us, our little destination was in full view. Edward veered off the trail (before reaching the teahouse) and down a short scree slope into the valley. We then laboured across the glacier to a lengthy steep section covered with gravel-like stones. Finally we came within the vicinity of the three peaks and travelled southeast, away from the steep cliffs of Mount Lefroy and toward the Mitre. Soon we arrived at the bottom of the pass, which is a steep, narrow ribbon of glacier between the Mitre and Mount Aberdeen. At this point we roped up: Edward first, then Pat, followed by me, Michael, Cindy and Mike – the anchor on the end. In the more than 25 years that had elapsed since Edward had been up this pass, its chute-like form had steepened considerably due to general recession of the glacier. Nevertheless, we were thrilled to be on this steep terrain with Edward and I thought we were all doing well. Both the nadir and the zenith of this outing occurred close to the summit of the pass.

All at once, rocks started tumbling down the pass from the peak opposite us, Mount Aberdeen. Edward yelled for us to run for cover. Michael and I were able to quite easily retreat behind a band of rock with our hands clasped behind our necks and our forearms over our ears, just like "drop drills" in school. Cindy and Mike were less well protected. Pat and Edward – above us all on the slopes – were completely out in the open, but the rocks seemed to be coming mostly toward the four of us below. I remember the sharp *crack!* as rocks landed on the ledges just above our heads and then bounced thuddingly on their way. I do not know how many just flew over us. Probably the cracking and thudding was over in just a few seconds, but like all such experiences, it seemed much longer.

Thinking the slide was over, I peeked over the edge of our rock band just in time to see another rock, about four inches in diameter, about the size of a croquet ball, headed straight for my mother. My brother and I saw it bounce quite high on the slope above her, and in that split second there was a desperate, sickening awareness that it would hit her on the head and there would be nothing we could do about it. We just crouched there, stunned.

What happened next seemed miraculous. Edward leaned forward, ice axe in hand, with its metal tip parallel to the slope. Lunging toward the stone, he struck it with a quick jab – like a fencer – square on and with enough force to deflect it from its path. Pat was safe, but all I could think of in the moment was that the quick reflexes and decisive behaviour I had just witnessed were certainly not in the skill set of most 84-year-old grandfathers. Of course, being up on that glacier was not a usual expectation of most octogenarians either.

Once the immediate danger was over, Edward urged us upward, wanting us out of this terrain. Where one series of rocks had come down unexpectedly, he felt others were likely to follow. In the interim, Cindy had been struck on her hand by a small rock and was bleeding. Mike wanted to stop and patch it up then and there, but Edward, quickly assessing the wound as a "scratch," insisted on moving quickly up to the top of the pass. Of course, this was exactly the right thing to do. Lingering longer in the area would have courted danger. And going back down, with our backs to the slopes, would have been idiotic, especially given we were close to the top. Amidst considerable drama, as Mike was arguing we should go down, it was only with Edward's dogged determination that we arrived at the 8,450-foot (2575-metre) pass safely, albeit with Cindy still leaving small red droplets in the snow.

Once Cindy's hand was attended to, we sat in relative silence with our backs against the cool rock of the Mitre, barely nibbling our cheese sandwiches. The atmosphere was quite sombre, both figuratively and literally, as low clouds had settled in to match our moods. There was not much said about the incident, but Mike's continued angst over his daughter's near miss was palpable. I wondered if Michael and I were the only ones to have witnessed Edward's deflection of the rock.

After lunch it was decided we would descend the opposite side of the pass, which was less steep and not glaciated. We negotiated our way down a considerable amount of scree and came to a small, relatively low-angled seasonal cascade lined with shrubbery. Edward began bounding down beside the water. His departure was a signal for us all to follow quickly before he got too far ahead. We did. I remember again admiring Edward's agility, as I, a reasonably nimble teenager, found the slope to be awkward going. I could feel water from the cascade sprinkling my face periodically as we made our way downward for several hundred metres before veering off onto the talus-covered slope. We were much more

fatigued, as it was the end of the day, which made negotiating the rubble tedious. Eventually we crossed the upper
portion of the Paradise Valley trail and headed down to
the trailhead – more than six kilometres away – past the
once well-known cascades called the Giant Steps.

It may come as a complete surprise that there are actually mosquitoes in Paradise, but they are there in abundance and they are really large – at least they were that
year. Once Edward's feet hit the trail, he lit his pipe and
puffed furiously in self-defence. Cindy and I did our best
to walk close behind him so we could take advantage of
the billowing smoke. It was some protection from the
insects that swarmed us as we plodded out the last few
monotonous kilometres. Needless to say, by the end of
this outing we were all thoroughly exhausted and at risk
of falling face down in our post-event bowl of soup.

The five of us had very sore muscles the next day.
Predictably, Edward was physically fine. He was emotionally shaken by the rockfall incident, though. When
he told Martha about it, his tone was restrained and sombre. He realized it had been a close call. However, these
are the risks of travelling in the mountains. Nothing even
Edward could have done would have prevented that slide.
Fortunately we would have numerous other glacier travels with Edward, but none of them would be as dramatic
as this one had been.

As a postscript to the emotional saliency engendered
by the Mitre Pass incident, Martha remarked in a letter to J. Monroe Thorington, dated September 20, 1968,
"Edward went with a family of five over Mitre Pass in

July; but had a very serious experience which might have turned into a sad tragedy. Two huge Rocks came rolling fast over the Snow to Glacier; fortunately, he managed to shout and warn the party to run for safety under a Rock band."[126] Of particular interest in her account is that while she mentioned Edward's role in shouting a warning, she omitted the quick actions which likely saved Pat's life. Perhaps he never told her. What I do know is that although she worried about her aging husband's compulsion for adventure (as most partners would), the incident did not sour her relationship with us in the least.

❉ ❉ ❉

The shrill whistle of the siffleur
first pierces the silence…

— WALTER WILCOX, *THE ROCKIES OF CANADA* (1909).

Edward, bending forward with a bit of sandwich in his hand and with real gentleness in his voice, called, "Jimmy! Jimmy!" A small, furry creature approached cautiously and snatched the offering. However, not lacking in manners entirely, and no doubt wishing to demonstrate his gratitude, he sat only a few feet away on his haunches holding the food to his mouth with his little black, hand-like forepaws. Although Edward had hunted for food and sport in his younger years, he remarked that he had gotten "tender-hearted" in his old age and did not like to think of killing animals.

The Îyârhe Nakoda name for the little creature, as translated into English, is "whistler." Standing over two feet tall on its haunches, and weighing eight to 15 pounds (3.6 to 6.8 kilograms), this is the most charismatic of the mountain rodents. Anyone who would abhor such a description of a rodent has never met a hoary marmot. Their clear, high, monotone whistle sounds as if they are welcoming visitors to their alpine home. It is, of course, a warning to their comrades to duck into their boulder-protected burrows. Marmots have many dreadful enemies – both on the ground and in the air – eager to claim them as lunch.

Why all marmots were "Jimmy" was never clear to me, but they were. Edward felt it was all right to feed these charming residents of high alpine valleys to help them survive the winter. "Soon they go to sleep and don't wake up until next May," he told us. Of course, the feeling about that sort of thing – feeding snacks to wild animals – has changed today and rightly so.

❊ ❊ ❊

I still hope to see you in the Canadian
Rockies again some day and that I
may take you for a brisk walk.

— EDWARD, IN A LETTER
TO J. MONROE THORINGTON, MAY 25, 1952

After Edward retired from the CPR, many guests he had climbed with during his long career, while older themselves, were still wanting to go on trips. He climbed with some of them throughout his 70s. He also enjoyed backpacking trips, and in addition to camping he spent as much as a month each year with guests at Temple Lodge or in the relative luxury of Lake O'Hara Lodge.

Rudi Gertsch, two generations younger than Edward, tells of descending a trail at Lake O'Hara after guiding a climb. Far below he saw a small puff of smoke. And then another. Rudi thought to himself, "This could only mean one thing." Sure enough, a few moments later he could see Edward coming up the trail, with his guests lagging far behind. When Edward caught up to him, Rudi sent his party ahead and the two guides sat down to have a little chat and a nip or two while they waited for Edward's party – now "old and slow," he moaned – to catch up to him.

On another occasion, when Edward was well into his 80s, we had travelled several kilometres carrying packs with overnight gear. After we pitched the tents, four of them, the skies darkened and rain mixed with hail began pelting down. Tea that evening was served in the rain. Although it can be boring sitting in a pup tent in the rain, you can always play cards or read and later make a dash to all the other tents proffering a flask of brandy to the rain-weary.

❄ ❄ ❄

The tents for the accommodation for the large number of members attending were pitched beside a fringe of trees, at the head of a grassy hanging valley, just under a well-timbered spur of Mount Niles and enclosed between two branches of Sherbrooke Creek.

— ALPINE CLUB OF CANADA,
"REPORT OF THE 1911 CAMP"[127]

The hike to Sherbrooke Lake is easy, on a trail which traverses along the east side of the lake. Reaching the inlet of the lake, Edward, who appeared vigilant, was acutely aware that this was the location where, decades before, his friend Chrigel Häsler and Nicholas Morant, the CPR photographer, had surprised a female grizzly bear and were mauled. It was at this point that the group spent a few minutes before finding a reasonable way to navigate across to the correct side of Sherbrooke Creek, ultimately using a log to do so. Having arrived at the steep ravine that was their only way forward, they were confronted with a jumble of shrubbery and an assortment of fallen trees piled high. Perhaps the result of an avalanche or a tremendous flood, the mass of fallen trunks and branches blocked their path for as far forward as they could see. Most members of the party assumed they would give up on the goal of camping in the meadows below Mount Niles. It looked too difficult – for all reasonable intents and purposes, impassable.

But Edward, now aged 88, was not to be deterred by the inconvenience of this barrier, never mind ghostly grizzly bears. He moved forward and upward, not only finding a way but negotiating the seemingly endless tangle with more energy and determination than the rest of his small group and certainly not showing any deficits in strength or coordination. Anyone who has had to contend with terrain of this sort, not to mention while travelling uphill, would acknowledge that the going is slow and exhausting. They stepped over logs where possible, not always sure what sort of ankle-breaking hole might be on the other side. Others they sat on and swung their legs over; still others they crawled under, sometimes having to remove their backpacks. Some impassable tangles forced them to take long detours on the side of the hill. Edward, unhappy with his performance, remarked that he had lost his sense of balance. This was catastrophic thinking on his part. Cindy, who was following directly behind him, saw him miscalculate and inadvertently step into a hole only a couple of times. The other members of the party, who were one or two generations younger than he, did nowhere near as well.

Grateful to finally emerge from the ravine, the group continued on into an open valley until they found a likely-looking camping spot with Mount Niles above them. Then Edward said to Cindy, pointing matter-of-factly, "Go down to that tree and bring back the bucket." Looking quizzical, she nevertheless obeyed and found the tree. She returned carrying a bucket, which she was instructed to fill with water for tea, lunch and cleaning up.

It turned out that the bucket had been hanging on the very same nail since 1911, when the Alpine Club of Canada had held one of its annual summer climbing camps between two branches of Sherbrooke Creek. Edward referred to the bucket as if it had been placed there yesterday. Of course, he was acutely cognizant of the vast number of years that had gone by since the bucket had been left there, especially when worrying that he should have been performing better in his log-hopping. There were other moments, even for those who did not have memories of 1911, when what is present and what is long past seemed almost to merge. Bucket in hand, it was easy for Cindy to imagine herself coming back into camp from a long day of climbing in the company of a 26-year-old Edward, greeting people she felt she knew but had never met, all enjoying the extraordinary civility of having retired to the tea tent for a piece of pie. If the tangible object, the bucket, had not been where Edward told her to fetch it from, the moment would not have evoked the same poignancy. It might even have been forgotten.

❋ ❋ ❋

He loves to talk [to] the mountains
as well as to climb them.

— DON M. WOOD, 1947, *FÜHRER-BUCH*

On August 4, 1966, the *Calgary Herald* proclaimed: "Eighty-two-year-old Edward Feuz of Golden, BC, has climaxed a 60-year career as an alpine guide by leading the first party this year to cross the treacherous Abott's Pass between Lake O'Hara and Lake Louise."[128] This feat was accomplished with Henry Kingman along with Kingman's son and two grandsons. Henry had first climbed with Edward in 1906 at Glacier House, when he was a mere boy of 12, despite the protestations of his father, who had had a mountaineering accident while climbing in the Swiss Alps and was understandably uneasy about giving his consent. Many years later, in 1936 to be precise, Edward introduced Kingman's boys and also his wife to climbing at Lake O'Hara.[129] Now, at age 72,

Kingman took a last trip with his old friend and mentor. How proud he must have been.

In 1970 another old friend, fellow guide Bruno Engler, agreed to produce a documentary film about Edward for the CBC television series *This Land*. The two of them, along with Rudi Gertsch, were to be flown in to Lake O'Hara by the already legendary helicopter pilot Jim Davies. Edward was wary about helicopters, which was no wonder given his age and the fact that he had never flown in anything, wingless or otherwise. But with his usual forthright manner, he walked right up to the machine and grumbled, "Does this contraption fly?" Soon he would be singing the virtues of helicopters in the mountains and rejoicing that "the hard, plodding days are done – through all that terrible bush."

On the trail to Lake Oesa, which is the starting point for the non-glaciated route over Abbot Pass, Bruno filmed Edward demonstrating how to step very precisely in hobnail boots in order to achieve maximum friction on wet rock. While it was all fine and good to demonstrate a few basic mountaineering skills, Edward quickly grew impatient, feeling he was wasting his time down low. Acceding to his wish to get higher, they flew him up to Victoria Glacier and landed the helicopter right on the pass. Edward marvelled at the bird's-eye view from the helicopter, but after landing, ecstatic to be on Abbot Pass again, he immediately grabbed his ice axe and began demonstrating how to cut steps in the snow as Bruno filmed him. It did not take much imagination to see he was headed directly toward the vertical rocky pinnacle that stands on the pass, a spire which, on its southern side, drops off sharply all the way back down into Lake Oesa. Both Bruno and Rudi were apprehensive about Edward's intentions. They had reason to worry.

Reaching the pinnacle, Edward demonstrated how to put an ice axe into the snow to secure it and immediately began climbing up the rock. Rudi, who was a very young guide at the time, moved toward the pinnacle, but Edward rebuffed him with, "Step back, you greenhorn. I've been here many a time." Rudi acquiesced and Edward kept climbing. He arrived at the very small summit, and showing no issues with balance at all, stood up on top. What he did next caught his witnesses by surprise. Taking off his hat, he began to say his farewells: "Goodbye, Victoria; goodbye, Lefroy," and so on, saluting all the mountains around him. Edward's farewell was a natural thing for him to do and reflected genuine feeling; he had not anticipated being so high up and amongst the mountains again. Both of the younger guides, themselves a generation apart, were overcome with emotion. Bruno was shaking so badly that he had trouble holding the camera still, and Rudi fought back tears. The respect Edward had for the mountains, which to him were almost like family, made a profound impression on the younger guides, and telling the story decades later still caused emotion to rise in them.

Bruno and Rudi, witnessing Edward's goodbyes to his beloved mountains, understood his passion, but I wonder what feelings were generated in viewers when the Edward episode of *This Land* was first shown in 1971.

Did they think it was put on, or did they understand his genuine love of mountains? As Don Wood noted in 1947, Edward talked to mountains as a matter of course, just as he talked to animals and even trees. He also talked for years afterward about his thrilling helicopter ride to Abbot Pass, but it was not quite goodbye.

In the summer of 1973 I received a telephone call in Los Angeles from Mike, who had already arrived in Canada with Pat and Cindy. I had made the grim decision that it would be prudent to stay home that year in order to earn money for university. The call, from a pay phone, changed all that. Dad informed me that Edward was going over Abbot Pass in a few days and asked whether I could get there. What a question. Hanging up from this call and buzzing with single-minded determination, I immediately made another call, to the employer who'd just hired me for a summer job, and told them I had to quit before I'd even started. Edward, almost 89 years of age, was going over Abbot Pass. Summer jobs were irrelevant. I packed my rucksack and got on the first available bus that very evening, gripping my ice axe. Two days and several sleazy bus stations later, I was hitchhiking to the campground where my parents and sister were staying, not having slept a wink and probably not having eaten much either.

Climbing onto the bus for the short ride to Lake O'Hara, we were all too excited to speak. On arrival we rushed off the bus, threw on our packs and in no time at all were at Lake Oesa, some 200 metres higher than Lake O'Hara. As a hiking guidebook from the era poetically put it:

"Set within a high, barren cirque, beneath the towering spine of the Continental Divide, Lake Oesa is one of the more exquisite of the turquoise gems found above Lake O'Hara."[130] At the far end of this lake the rocky alpine ascent to Abbot Pass begins.

Edward, who had no difficulties whatsoever on this trip, was relaxed and clearly enjoying himself. We stopped partway up for a short rest in a rock shelter, and at 9,588 feet (2922 metres) Edward had again reached the pass, this time under his own steam, unlike three years earlier. Showing no overt signs of fatigue, he climbed the pinnacle on the pass (for what did turn out to be the last time) and urged Cindy and me to do so with him. We spent the afternoon high up with the hawks, relaxing in the sun and gazing at the impressive face of Mount Victoria, with its long summit ridge, almost 2,000 feet above us.

On September 9, 1909, Edward and Rudolf had made the first north to south traverse of Mount Victoria's ridge with G.W. Culver, who described the experience as almost 30 hours of incessant work. Although they made it to the north summit by ten in the morning, their progress thereafter was both slow and laborious. Frequently needing to travel on rotten rock, they also had to climb around a seemingly endless number of jagged pinnacles. At one point they found themselves at the edge of a steep drop-off, staring at the ridge some 60 feet below and quickly realizing they had no option but to lower down to it. Eventually the rock on the ridge improved, but they still did not arrive at the south peak (or main summit) until 7:00 in the evening. It had taken them nine hours to travel between the two peaks, and they still had to get down.

According to Culver,[131] within another hour it was "pitch black," which necessitated having to wait in a precarious and cold place for the moon to crest over the ridge of Mount Lefroy. Unfortunately it was only a quarter moon and a dim one at that, and because the snow on the descent was frozen, they needed to chop steps. Meanwhile a breeze developed, intermittently extinguishing the candles in their lanterns. By 2:30 the next morning they had managed to climb down to Abbot Pass. However, there was no hut there in those days, which meant they had to continue down the pass and stagger onward to the hotel, where they arrived in time for breakfast, which was no doubt of epic proportions. Writing in Edward's *Führer-Buch*, Culver stated, "The qualities that he there displayed were beyond reproach, and in my own mind have placed him on a standing far beyond that of the average guide."

Sixty-four years after his trip with Culver, Edward was again on Abbot Pass, but in a very crowded hut. After dinner Mike pulled some chairs into a corner near the door, away from all the noise. Edward, who was beaming, sat in a chair right under an old photo of himself (taken by Georgia Engelhard) leading on the snowy ridge of Mount Victoria toward the main peak. He had climbed to the south summit dozens of times in his life, taking a route which begins on the rocky ridge directly behind the proper Swiss-style mountain hut that Edward had promoted and helped build so many years before. Sheltered

224

within the same solid stone walls, he had a right to proprietary feelings.

That night, the four of us, who were packed in like sardines on a lower bunk, managed to sleep. Cindy, who was near the kitchen, was kept awake by a group of people who felt it was appropriate to make pancakes in the middle of the night. It turned out that Cindy was lucky, because she was lying awake when Pat walked by and was able to join her on a trip to the precariously perched "facilities." Once outside the hut Pat and Cindy experienced a crystal-clear night sky unpolluted by man-made light and crowded with dancing stars which, in the poetic sense, really did feel close enough to touch. They stood and stared in wonder until the frigid night air forced them inside.

Early the next day, following a hastily consumed and probably inadequate breakfast, we roped up and began descending the glaciated side of the pass toward Lake Louise. Starting down from the hut can be quite intimidating. Edward, having noticed Pat taking her first fear-filled look at the steep descent, kept her close to him. She gazed in respectful awe at gaping crevasses, and at other times tried to keep from thinking about the fact that she was walking across some of them on snow bridges. Mostly she was glad she did not have to linger. After passing safely out of the "Death Trap," where he had once been cemented in snow, Edward turned his head back toward the pass and Pat heard him say, "Fooled you again!"

The timing of our family's excursions north was fairly predictable. We usually planned to arrive in Golden around the middle of July, because that was the surest bet for settled weather. For some reason none of us can now recall, in the summer of 1974 we were late. Per the usual pattern, Edward and Martha were waiting for us, speculating over cups of tea when we would finally show up and wondering what was keeping us so long. But Martha, now 91, could not wait much longer.

We arrived that year to a very solemn-looking Edward, who, before breaking into sobs, managed to choke out a few words. Martha had died, he said, only one week before we arrived. We stood silent. Shocked. With the denial of youth, it had not crossed any of our minds that she would not be there. Moreover, age and other statistics are impersonal, useful only when making scientific prognostications about strangers; this was *Martha*.

To say it was a sad, difficult summer would be to trivialize the depths of Edward's sorrow at losing his life partner. But as mountain people cope with their grief by seeking the healing balm of nature, this was not a summer of passive grieving. As would be expected, he felt an almost constant need to review events from the past and to just talk about Martha, his rosy-cheeked girl. He had sympathetic listeners, even though the youngest member of the group was surprised at the intensity of his grief. But Cindy came to appreciate that Edward's capacity for deep emotional expressiveness added a more fallible and tender aspect to what could appear an indomitable facade, and it helped her redefine her own notions of strength. But the most stunningly poignant moment for our family came when Edward revealed that Martha's last words had been, "Give the Stephens a good time." After saying this, she simply shut her eyes and was gone. Of course, this was not about us. It was about Martha knowing that going out into the mountains with people who cared deeply about him would be the best of all possible ways for Edward to cope with losing her.

The most memorable trip that summer was an overnight excursion with just sleeping bags and "a little grub." Mike had wanted to bring tents, but Edward dismissed the idea, insisting they could make a shelter if it rained. So Pat, Mike and Cindy took a trip with Edward from Moraine Lake to the glaciated Wenkchemna Pass, a fairly long walk for the average hiker. They then continued on, over the pass, to Eagle's Eyrie. There they spent the night on the ground close to a large outcropping of rocks. Just as they were settling in, an electrical storm began threatening from the northeast. Edward leapt into action. He found a boulder which offered some protection and was far enough away from the pass to avoid rockfall, and then supervised the others as they scurried around looking for branches of just the right size to complete the roof. Soon they were comfortably waiting out the storm in their makeshift shelter, having previously supped, quite sumptuously they thought. In retrospect they were woefully malnourished, on meagre portions of cold meat, cheese, a couple of hard rolls and a handful of raisins. Later that night, a second lightning shower pelted the intrepid campers and again they dashed to their shelter, where they endured a significant downpour for almost an hour. Awakening to an innocently sunny day, they travelled over another glaciated pass, Opabin, to Lake O'Hara. Edward was almost 90 years old.

Showing up at the lodge in time for lunch, Edward was absorbed in sharing memories of Martha. There were several old-timers there to help console him. He introduced Cindy to everyone he knew and to some people he did not know, proudly exclaiming: "She's going to be a very good climber."

Retrospectively, it is clear that Edward fulfilled Martha's wish that year. He gave us a good time and began to heal ever so slightly. She was in our hearts and minds that summer and continues to be to this day as a woman of intelligence and determination but most of all a friend who added a special kindness and civility to our lives. Living in an era when we dash off terse, sometimes ambiguous messages on convenient electronic devices, a special memory of her is that she took the time to answer the letters of a child and even wrote a few in German so that I could practise. Her holiday card was always the first to arrive, almost unerringly, on the first day of December. It is astonishing to imagine now, with all the people they had known over decades, how large a group of correspondents she must have had.

❋ ❋ ❋

Now we'll be together, always.

— EDWARD

Our heavy packs laden with overnight gear, Edward, Mike, Pat, Uncle Frank and I wended our way through the forlorn foundations of Glacier House, the cozy CPR hotel in the wilderness that had been torn down in 1929. Originally built as a cabin to serve meals to passengers on the Atlantic and Pacific transcontinental trains, Glacier House became the first centre of alpinism in North America, at a time when the Great Glacier extended right into the forest.[132] It was the locale where Edward spent many summers taking tourists up the glaciers and ascending the peaks which rise above them. On this occasion, we were beginning a trek to the glaciated Asulkan Pass so that Edward, now 92, could peer across at Mount Dawson for "the last time." This mountain was special to him and travelling to see it was another mountain pilgrimage.

Mount Dawson is a huge, snow-covered massif, 11,079 feet in elevation (3377 metres), which cannot be glimpsed from the road. Edward's father and his friend Christian Häsler Sr. had made the first ascent of this peak on August 13, 1899 – their first season in Canada – guiding professors Charles Fay and Herschel C. Parker. Fay and Parker asked the guides' impressions as to its relative difficulty. They rated it as being as hard as Sir Donald and harder than the Matterhorn but similar to the Wetterhorn. At Fay's suggestion, and with Parker's enthusiastic seconding of the idea, the two peaks were subsequently named Häsler and Feuz. Fay enthused, "These splendid specimens of their craft deserve a lasting memorial in these scenes which they are rendering accessible to so many."[133]

Several years later, in 1905, Feuz Sr., along with the young Edward, guided the auspicious Swami Abhedānanda, of Kolkata, up the peak. The latter, a devotee of the mystic Ramakrishna, was a handsome and immensely popular teacher during the wave of Vedic interest which first swept North America just prior to the onset of the 20th century. Herschel Parker, an amateur climber as noted above, was a physicist at Columbia University. He was also a member, indeed at one time the president, of the Vedanta Society – followers of Ramakrishna – which probably accounts for the swami's presence in the Selkirk Mountains six seasons after the first ascent. Surely, guiding a Hindu holy man was a uniquely exotic and memorable experience for a young Swiss fellow.

So there we were, decades later, headed for Mount Dawson. Gaining considerable altitude, we came to a small clearing beside the Asulkan River. We camped at a site Edward had used many times before, including once on a trip with William Randolph Hearst and six "office girls." They did not climb any peaks, but it was probably an exciting outing for them to be in the Canadian wilderness in a tent. We can assume it was exciting, because just after the group had retired, Hearst rushed back to Edward, still sitting by the campfire, to ask if he would sleep with the girls, who had their own bell tent, because they were worried about a bear. Edward had pointed out a bear far across the valley earlier that day, and the women were nervously obsessed with the sighting. By nightfall they were convinced the bear was going to sneak up on them as they slept! Hearst's motivation in asking for Edward was probably one of "propriety," but Edward laughed heartily at the request. Yes, he told Hearst, he would be very happy to sleep with the girls.

Having emerged from our own tents, with clouds overhead, we began our way up the trail to a high spine of lateral moraine which flanked the glacier on its east side. We then followed a narrow trail along the crest of the spine. As two other parties were making their way to the toe of the glacier far below us, Edward stopped for an instructional moment. He pointed out to us how the terrain on the opposite side of the glacier was subject to avalanche risk, making the climbers below vulnerable. Thus it was a better choice, he said, to gain access to the glacier higher up as we were doing. We continued on the narrow trail until Edward came to the place where he decided we would make our descent onto the glacier. There we roped up. After we had traversed upward for a time, it started sleeting. Wind from the south blew stinging pellets into our faces. As the two other parties were making hasty retreats down the glacier, we moved quickly and with purpose in the opposite direction, toward the pass, where Edward was beckoned by his memories. He reached the pass and stood on top for a time in silence, gazing at the mist-shrouded mountain. Finally he pointed out Feuz Peak, which, he said with pride, was named for "dad."

Although the senior Feuz was not perfect, Edward had deep admiration and respect for his father and no doubt missed him. After Edelweiss Village was built, CPR-sponsored trips to Europe had ended. Consequently, the last time Edward had seen either of his parents, or his homeland, was 1912. By the time he showed us Feuz Peak, both parents had been gone for decades and Switzerland was quite different from the place of his youth. Mike had tried to cajole him into returning for a visit after Martha died. Although Edward was seriously tempted, he ultimately decided that too much would have changed in more than 60 years. It was better to avoid the sense of estrangement he might have felt.

The pilgrimage to Dawson was a success, even though Edward had wanted to continue down the other side of the pass to get as close to his memories as possible. Unfortunately the weather was too poor to continue, and by this time there was an electrical storm brewing. Still, Edward looked content and happy when he turned away and shouted, "We'd better go to beat the band!" Maybe he had been thinking of Swami Abhedānanda's kind words describing Edward and his dad as "excellent guides on rock, snow and ice and very careful in most difficult and dangerous places."[134]

By the time we reached the top of the rocky spine above the glacier, Edward chose to descend off the trail so Frank would not be intimidated by the changed character of the narrow trail, now muddy and with slippery stones mixed in for added challenge and excitement. Plus, it was very windy and Edward was worried about us being blown off. Meanwhile, snowflakes gradually turned into a Scottish mist. And Scottish it looked, with the overcast sky and rough, heather-covered hillocks. Frank balked at leaving the trail, but he was told it was a better choice despite the added effort required. Edward, Mike and I had bounded down over the uneven terrain while Pat stayed behind to accompany Frank, who was by far the slowest member of our little group. The three in the advance group stopped and waited for the rearguard to catch up as Pat and Frank, in long, hooded ponchos and carrying alpenstocks, solemnly wound their way down the hill, still some distance away. Edward watched them for a minute, grinning. We wondered what he was thinking. Obviously having been transported back to a moment from his youth, he quipped, "They look like nuns!" And, so they did.

It poured rain all that night. Our tents leaked and I ended up sleeping in a puddle. Pat was more stoic about the situation than I was, but Edward and Mike, who were sharing a tent, seemed undisturbed. We could hear their whispered conversations until late in the night. By mid-morning the rain was not letting up at all, and we decided to strike camp and get out of there. Packing up was a miserable experience, but it at least offered some hope of respite, albeit after a long hike. After I had packed up most of our gear, I noticed Edward was standing beside his tent struggling to untie one of the knots on a guy line. Imagining that his fingers were cold – mine certainly were – and guessing they felt fairly stiff besides, I moved up beside him, discreetly took the line out of his hand so no one would see, and untied the knot. Mike and I then surreptitiously removed as much gear as we could from Edward's pack, without making it appear obvious that we had done so, and divided it between us.

The sodden condition of our tents and sleeping bags, plus the extra load, made our packs much heavier than they had been on the way in. The abundance of exotic, waist-high shrubbery, typical of these mountains, was of course wet and added to the overall discomfort. Focused on the goal – a dry vehicle – we tramped out in glum silence, Edward in the lead as always. Arriving at the trailhead, our journey finally at an end, Edward roared, "That was one hell of a walk!"

We know Edward was proud of his accomplishment that year because he mentioned it to someone who had come to interview him in the autumn. People understandably wanted to talk about the past with Edward. Even though he was frequently happy to do so, he also did not like being treated as if he were just a repository of mountaineering history. He was, after all, alive and in the present. What he was doing in the present may not have had historical interest for others, but Edward enjoyed his time in the mountains no matter how old he was, and he did some amazing things given the age at which he did them. So when an interviewer asked him when he had stopped guiding, he responded, sounding quite exasperated, "I'm *still* guiding."

While Edward's dad and Christian Häsler Sr. had peaks on Mount Dawson named for them after only a relatively brief time in Canada, getting peaks named for the second generation of CPR Swiss guides – who were equally famous and historically important – proved to be quite difficult. The prejudice seemed to have been that they had been acknowledged enough, which was simply not true. They had no tangible recognition, and their individual legacies were in danger of morphing into a concept of the generic "Swiss guide," a danger which I fear has been taken up increasingly by various marketing efforts as the years go by.

Thankfully, in 1970, their case was enthusiastically put forward by Sydney Vallance, a former president of the Alpine Club of Canada who, as a barrister, was willing to battle red tape. Initially it was proposed that some of the guides be acknowledged by christening two peaks in a well-known and easily accessible region. For his part, Edward was very much in favour of acknowledging all five second-generation Swiss guides and suggested the Lyells, on the boundary between Alberta and British Columbia. Although not easily accessible, they had the advantages of being exactly the right number and being big peaks – each over 11,000 feet. Further, they had always been referred to by number (one through five) rather than by specific names. Edward had made first ascents on three of these and Ernst on one of them. Finally, it was agreed that the peaks would be named for all five guides, and they would be known by the guides' anglicized first names (rather than their last names), thus avoiding confusion with Feuz and Häsler peaks in the Selkirks. They are now known in the order Edward favoured: Rudolph Peak, Edward Peak, Ernest Peak, Walter Peak and Christian Peak. Sadly, Ernst and Christian had not lived long enough to see this honour bestowed.

To commemorate the event, Bruno Engler combined two photos he had taken, one showing the five guides at Lake Louise, the other with "their peaks" above them.

He presented a copy of the montage to Edward, who was thrilled to finally have his own peak.

"We were together all those years; now we'll be together always,"[135] he enthused.

CHAPTER 9

LIFE WITH EDWARD

Edward was fond of our uncle Frank. He appreciated his patient, artistic approach to photography and the fact that despite Frank's failure to attain a trim physique, he was game for adventure. Frank was not born with an impulse to wander. Most of his exploits in life had been of the armchair variety. So it was a surprise when, in his middle years, he finally yielded to his younger brother's cajoling and took his first trip out west – all the way from Montreal by train. He came with his wife, who was svelte and urbane. After meeting the couple for the first time, Edward, true to his irreverent sense of humour, mischievously suggested they try "going a few rounds" after supper.

Teenagers frequently project an aura of disdain when subjected to adults saying outrageous things, a sadly transparent attempt to mask their constant fear of embarrassment. To my sister and me, the boxing match suggestion was comical. We could imagine the couple duking it out – throwing and blocking uppercuts, hooks, jabs and roundhouse blows. But especially amusing was the image of our fashion-conscious aunt, bobbing and weaving, her coiffed hair staying resolutely stationary.

Frank was impressed with Edward, who, always eager to introduce novices to the enchantment of his world, included Frank on hikes which were easy enough for him to accomplish. After the sad and untimely death of his wife, Frank made half a dozen trips to the mountains, graduating to backpacking, but never managed to sweat off more than a few pounds. Each year after returning home to the city, he sent copies of his best photographs to Edward and was proud to call him a friend.

At times when there were six or more adults (including two semi-adults) at Martha and Edward's house, tensions would occasionally arise. All of them were fairly trivial: Cindy and I were able to quickly demonstrate to Edward that the alarming-looking black pot marks we had made while washing dishes in the porcelain kitchen sink were not permanent. But Frank, probably due to the proximity of his usual sleeping quarters – on the screened back porch – was the scapegoat for some of Edward's own kitchen mishaps. One forgotten kettle, its bottom burned out, was attributed to Frank having got up in the middle of the night to make a cup of tea. Frank strenuously proclaimed his innocence, but to no avail. He should help himself, Edward reassured him, but he should also try to remember to turn off the stove.

Realizing with a groan that it was seven-something in the morning, Cindy and I both had the overtired, hungover feeling that can result from strenuous exertion the day before and too little sleep. Edward, who had been asleep when we came in at midnight from our long climb on

Mount Sir Donald, was now engaged in some noisy activity in the room next to ours. We had awakened to pacing and thumping sounds, as if he were carrying heavy boxes from one side of the basement to the other and then dropping them. For a brief moment we were baffled, unable to imagine what he could possibly be doing. Finally it dawned on us that the intent of the racket was to assist us with waking up because he was anxious to find out whether we had made it to the summit of the mountain. We responded to the noise by squeezing our eyes shut, desperately trying to drift back to sleep and hoping that if we just ignored him... Of course, our efforts were doomed because the production in the next room was in full swing. Literally.

After some time, realizing the failure of his stratagem and unable to tolerate the suspense any longer, he simply flung open our door, sending the doorknob crashing into a nearby table, and walked toward us. We feigned sleep while doing our best to repress laughter, which was easiest to do face down. Figuring we were very heavy sleepers, he leaned over us in turn, gently ruffling our hair and calling, "Cindy. Donna." We then "awakened" to a questioning face peering down at us: "Well, did you do it?" There was only ever one "it." We smiled and responded categorically "Yes." Breaking into a broad grin and with the pride of a proud papa, he exclaimed, "I knew you did!" and then hurried from the room. We later learned, only after he had sent a clipping, that he had gone to the local newspaper to brag about our success in hopes they would write an article, which they did. Although we were embarrassed that he had done this, since what we had achieved was not extraordinary, we were touched by his enthusiasm.

Not all of our climbs were successful, of course, and in those cases Edward's forthright style of communication was not always so tender. "I knew when you barfed, you wouldn't make it" is one remark that stays in my mind. Of course he was correct. Throwing up one's breakfast is never an especially good omen. Still, though we obviously preferred to bask in the afterglow of the successful efforts, even the failed attempts were more desirable than the misery of a valley socked in with clouds and deluged with torrents of rain. A day of sustained bad weather would try our collective patience, and our moods would become lugubrious. After all, there is only so much resting, reading, tea drinking and biscuit eating one can do.

Stuck in the house on stormy days, Edward would become restless. At some point he would jump up and begin pacing, mumbling in his distinctive low, grumbling sort of way. The end point of his perambulations was predictable. Eventually he would thud across the carpet and into the kitchen. But he always bypassed the fridge (the answer was not there) to stand before the barometer on the far wall. He would give the instrument two or three measured and gentle, one could even say reverent, taps. When preceded by a deep sigh, the pronouncement would be, "It's no good." Then Cindy and I would stride to the nearest window and crane our necks for signs of blue to contradict the reading. Such a portent of good weather would send all our hearts soaring with hope.

For a time, there was also a second barometer in Edward's house. Her name was Goldie. She was a sweet spaniel-type dog with long droopy ears, adoring brown eyes and a butterscotch-coloured coat. Although she was technically Gertie's dog, she kept Edward and Martha company, following them everywhere. Like some other dogs, Goldie had a special talent for weather forecasting, a second sense she probably wished she did not possess. Long before any obvious signs of a thunderstorm, Goldie would run down the basement steps and begin to quake with fear. It was a pitiful sight to behold. No amount of cajoling could get her out of the basement, and no amount of reassurance would ever calm her fear. She knew danger was on the way. Nothing could convince her otherwise.

Reaching the age of majority, or close to it, Cindy and I began making the trip to Edward's house and the mountains on our own. At first this meant long, uncomfortable bus rides, and later we were able to procure our own independent transportation. But I did not think Martha and Edward would like my new car. The only automobile they had ever owned – a dove-grey tank – was sitting in the garage. They had purchased the 1940 Chevy new and it was still pristine. My new pride and joy was a spunky British sports car, a Triumph TR6, painted the colour of Buddhist monks' robes. It was a two-seater convertible with a lovely tan interior and a jaunty luggage rack over a trunk that was deceptively large for the size of the car. But viewed with a sober eye, it was small, impractical and saffron coloured, so I was surprised when the two of them began falling over themselves complimenting the car. They didn't just like it. They beamed. "Oh, it's very nice," enthused Martha, who did not know how to drive and to my knowledge had never expressed any real interest in vehicles. Maybe the car truly was the colour of bliss.

Edward and Martha had lived through the mass-market introduction and popularization of vehicles, most of which seemed to come in your choice of colour as long as it was black. But I suppose something a little more astonishing was a welcome relief to the boring array of vehicles they had experienced. Other older friends of mine – even those who were disinclined to travel at speeds more dizzying than 50 kilometres per hour – were similarly enamoured of my diminutive, brightly coloured ride. So much for stereotypes.

Edward's own relationship to vehicles was one of strict utility and not vanity, cuteness or speed. In short, it should do what he wanted it to do without resistance. Once, impatient to check the fluid in the radiator and leaning over the still hot engine, he somehow managed to twist off the radiator cap. Not an easy thing to do. The consequence of this "success" was, of course, scalding his face. When we arrived later that same summer, he showed us some peeling skin, but by then most of the tangible evidence of the incident had miraculously vanished.

Edward was a speed demon on the highway. In town he just meandered, without any regard for which way traffic was supposed to travel, going wherever his whims took him. If he saw a good parking spot, he set out to claim it by the shortest possible route, legal or otherwise.

As teenagers we sat with as much stoicism as we could muster when Edward drove us around town, gritting our teeth and pretending we were not embarrassed by his brazen manoeuvres. Pugilistic aunties are one thing; devil-may-care grandpa drivers are quite another.

When the time came for the decision that he should no longer drive, Edward gave his car away. Then he bought transportation with two wheels. Unfortunately, like some other older adults I have known, this solution was short-lived. After the erstwhile happy cyclist found himself flying over the handlebars, a bike no longer seemed a practical alternative to a car. Fortunately, Edward was not injured in the fall, but from then on he was dependent on others for transportation. When it was feasible to do so, he walked.

Once close to the first of August, while we were carrying the breakfast dishes to the sink, Edward turned the page of the calendar which always hung next to the kitchen window, and pointed to the first square. This was *Bundesfeiertag* in Switzerland, he told us, a time of celebration, fireworks and bonfires on the summits of hills. Edward had fond memories of growing up in Interlaken and climbing trees to get the best view. I asked him if he remembered an *erste August* when Hans Lüscher had carried an enormous pack board of firewood to the summit of Fairview Mountain, a peak accessible by hiking, which overlooks Lake Louise. Indeed, he did. Fortunately he had been outside and looking up that night or he would not have seen Hans's surprise bonfire.

Lüscher, who was a good writer and amateur photographer, wound up as a cook's helper at the Chateau Lake

Louise in the mid-1920s. Hans had a tortuous inner life. His search for symbols and underlying meanings in the ordinary would have been perplexing to Edward, whose orientation toward life was simultaneously pragmatic and aesthetic. When things needed to be done or there were problems to be solved, analysis came into play. But when he exulted in a beautiful day, it was a happiness content with sensation; analysis was irrelevant.

Despite their differences in temperament, Edward felt sorry for the lonely Swiss boy – who had been an orphan – and took him under his wing. Hans had a terror of heights and experienced vertigo. Nevertheless, he taught himself to climb, on the cliffs behind the lake, by forcing himself to avoid looking down. As the world is a small place, Hans ended up living only two miles from us in Los Angeles 30 or more years later and became a good family friend. Edward introduced Hans and his wife to us while on a road trip to California with Swiss chef and hotelier Joe Zimmerman. After a requisite trip to watch oranges grow, and drives down various boulevards, the six adults had a night out at Old Heidelberg (the closest they could come to a Swiss restaurant), where they enjoyed copious quantities of German comfort food washed down with beer.

Another *Bundesfeiertag* was a cause of much embarrassment to Edward when the Royal Canadian Mounted Police arrived at his door and told him he could not fly his Swiss flag on this day or any other. Confronting him like this seemed like an unnecessarily mean thing to do to an old man who was just trying to maintain what was by then a very distant link to the home of his youth. Especially ironic was the fact that the CPR, as part of their marketing campaign, worked diligently to import as much "Swiss culture" as they could and insisted the Swiss flag be raised above Edelweiss Village every day. But decades later Edward was told to take the flag down, on this one special day. Cindy and I were so angry seeing how disheartened Edward was that we immediately marched off to the station to tell the police what we thought of this injustice, but there was no one there. Considering the adrenalin flowing on that brief walk, maybe it was just as well the station was locked up tight.

This was not the only time we acted in a protective manner toward Edward. Although climbers who were familiar with his name clamoured for the chance to shake his hand, an old man carrying an ice axe and dressed in old-fashioned climbing clothes would sometimes elicit smirking looks from the general public. On one occasion, walking by the front of the Chateau, we could see Edward was uncomfortable amongst the throngs of tourists, so instead of leaving him in the lead, we simply flanked him and glared at anyone who showed disrespect. Other times, Cindy would lag behind in order to tell such people that Edward was a very famous mountain guide and they should feel fortunate to have encountered him.

Edward, no longer capable of accompanying Cindy and me on climbs, went out and hired a guide for us so we could fulfill our aspirations to climb more serious peaks. It wasn't that he was advising against going out on our own; he just wanted to help us succeed on the more dangerous stuff. And thus it was that we were sitting at his kitchen table one evening waiting for this guide to arrive. It was one of those sweltering summer nights that is remembered in the dead of winter as having been languorously sweet, but Cindy and I were uncomfortable, perspiring and enveloped in a blue haze of tobacco smoke as we listened to Edward reminisce. As we waited, we wondered what this guide would be like.

Soon the screen door opened and in walked *the guide*. Instantly, I felt my jaw slacken and we all stared at each other, smiling idiotically – all of us except Edward. He sat Buddha-like, but with his twinkling eyes darting between Cindy and me, and the familiar little smile forming at the corners of his mouth. Well done, Edward, we thought. He had found us a guide, alright. He was tall, handsome, blond and blue-eyed, with a charming smile. Best of all, he was *Swiss*. It occurred to us that Edward had simply found a younger (and taller) version of himself; very considerate and generous, we thought. Following this eternal instant, Edward rose and made the introductions, "Donna, Cindy, this is your guide, Sepp Renner."*

---

* Sepp Renner was born in the mountain village of Andermatt in 1946. Enthralled with tales of wilderness he had read as a child, Sepp dreamed of coming to Canada. After receiving his guide certificate in the Bernese Oberland, in 1967, he did exactly that. Sepp first worked as a freelance mountain guide at Lake Louise, and then guided 13 years for Canadian Mountain Holidays. Between 1983 and 2010 Sepp and his wife, Barb, charmed hundreds of guests as proprietors of Assiniboine Lodge. Still seeking out high places, to date Sepp has made 54 ascents of Mount Assiniboine.

The rest of the brief meeting was a blur, but we went on to make a date with Sepp to climb Mount Victoria, Edward's first choice for us. Shortly after the meeting concluded, Edward approached us and asked coyly, "Well, did I do a good job?" We responded enthusiastically, but any response was really unnecessary. It was written all over our faces.

Returning from a long day tramping in the hills can leave one feeling not only tired but sometimes a little chilled, even in the summer months. This was why Edward favoured a warm, nutritious bowl of soup after outings. Sometimes this was followed by a cup of coffee and a piece of pie, preferably berry and heated up. We liked this habit, but as teenagers and young adults, we considered soup and pie to be just afternoon tea. Later in the day there would be a substantial dinner of hamburgers and a real milkshake, or two, or several pieces of roast chicken with baked potatoes and a salad fresh from the garden. Climbing gives one a voracious appetite.

Basements being partially below ground and having concrete walls, they of course stay cool and lovely on hot summer nights when such cave-like dwellings offer advantages. But when he thought we were looking chilled, Edward would march down the basement steps with determination, on a mission to light the dreaded gas heater in our room.

Crouched face down in front of the heater, Edward would be on all fours fumbling with various knobs. Concerned, realistically or not, about a gas explosion, we yelled at him because his back was turned to us and he was fairly hard of hearing in his later years. "Really, Edward, we're fine. It's okay, we don't need the heater," we pleaded, standing as far away as we could and still be in the same room. He brushed us off with a guttural grunt, as if to say "don't be silly, it's cold in here," while continuing to examine the heater in a determined manner. Finally he found the pilot-light switch and turned it on. We knew this because a menacing hissing sound was emanating from the ancient contraption. "Is it on?!" he yelled, his face still in the same vulnerable position. "Yes!" we shrieked, resisting the urge to run. Then he sat back on his haunches and in a leisurely manner struck a big wooden match. Our hearts stood still. An eternity later there was a loud *whoomp*. After making a few adjustments, Edward got up from the floor and showed us the controls. "Thank you," we quavered. "You're welcome," he said, leaving the room. As soon as he had gone, we opened the window...

Being the perfect host, Edward not only wanted us to be comfortable, he also wanted to help us fill our social and recreational calendar. Sometimes social opportunities arrived at the house – Lillian Gest or Lizzie Rummel or some other mountain person might drop by. Cindy and I tried to keep a few homemade cookies in the cupboard, so we would not be caught unprepared.

Lizzie Rummel,* was a real mountain woman and an extremely well-liked personage who had run several backcountry lodges. She had been awarded the Order of

* Elisabet von Rummel (1897–1980).

Canada for her environmental stewardship and enthusiastic promotion of Canadian mountain environments. Prior to Cindy and I meeting Lizzie for the first time, Edward told us, with a little awe in his voice, that her name was really *von* Rummel. She was a baroness who had been stranded in Canada with her family by the start of the First World War. She was not a peasant like the rest of us. Unfortunately, Edward introduced me to the baroness in German. I spewed my *dies, ders* and *dasses* with reckless abandon and probably little precision. It was not an impressive performance.

Lillian Gest* was also an interesting personage who came to tea. Well-educated, she had received an A.B. from Vassar and an A.M. in social work from the University of Pennsylvania. In an era when upper-class families typically imposed such restrictions on their daughters, she was forbidden to take a job. Thus she became a philanthropist and eventually vice-president of the Philadelphia Children's Aid Society.[136] Gest had first visited the Rockies with her mother in 1921, and eventually accumulated a total of fifty trips. She could often be found romping around the Lake O'Hara area (along with a gang of other older-generation climbers) and wrote historical pamphlets about this and other popular mountain places.

More often than waiting for visitors to come to us, Edward was on the phone begging after-dinner opportunities. Off we would all go – usually on foot – to his brother's, sister-in-law's or daughter's house for tea and

* Lillian Gest (1889–1986).

whatever baked goods they had stored for such occasions. Although we were embarrassed by Edward's boldness in securing such invitations, they were always memorable social occasions and frequently offered the prospect of connecting to more mountain history and lore. In addition there was usually a bit of bragging by Edward and the subjects of the tales would sit blushing uncomfortably. Then we would all traipse home, "giving the legs a good stretch," as Edward liked to say.

Once, we heard from a neighbour who had telephoned while we were out that Edward had said, "Yes, the girls are out playing pool and they'll probably stop by the pub for a beer before they come home." All wild conjecture on Edward's part of course, but there was really little to do in Golden in those days. There was not even a public pool. During an especially hot summer, Edward, anticipating our arrival, had gone to a local motel owner and asked if we could come over for a swim now and then. "Chutzpah," we thought, but appreciated nonetheless. On the subject of beer, we did go to the new pub in town, a big log cabin with a cheery atmosphere – not at all dingy in the way the word "bar" used to connote.

It was fairly late on a Saturday night when the three of us arrived and sat down at the only open table we could find. Edward was in a jovial mood and enthusiastically ordered "a big jug!" Upon hearing this, Cindy looked a little concerned because she was not much of a beer drinker and I was wildly trying to calculate how much beer I would have to consume. Edward was in his 90s, after all, and did not have the tolerance for large amounts of alcohol. And I knew he would not be happy, being of a perfectionist personality, until every drop was drained from the jug.

The atmosphere at the pub was loud that night, and after only half a glass of beer, Edward, thoroughly enjoying himself and clearly disinhibited, started singing *Bierstube* songs at the top of his powerful but not unpleasant voice. Normally this sort of thing would stop the house. People do not tend to sing spontaneously in North American pubs – no real *Kameradschaft*, as Edward would say – but much to my relief the din was too great for anyone to notice, and so I relaxed. From time to time he would wink, nudge me and ask, "Did you understand that one?" I would grin and say, "I think so..." We were having a grand time, but only *tête-à-tête* because Cindy was still nursing her original glass of beer. With persistence I had risen to the challenge and finished the jug. But instead of ending the evening – at least from the point of view of drinking – Edward hollered for another one, jug that is. I thought I was holding up rather well under the circumstance, but clearly my tactical appraisal of the situation had been flawed. Now I was faced with a second jug. Cindy, looking weary at this point, rose to excuse herself. "Where's Cindy going?" he asked, looking puzzled. "Home," I said, and added, fabricating, "she has a headache." Edward, again youthful, went on singing slightly suggestive ditties until the second jug was drained.

We emerged from the pub after midnight. One of us was weaving. Summoning up some courage, I boldly reached over and took Edward's arm in mine. He did not object and we marched purposefully down the eerily still lane. The whole town seemed to be asleep. Thankfully, Edward had stopped singing and instead was concentrating on walking. My intent was to look dignified, and if I couldn't achieve that, to at least appear normal, but my mind was whirring. I hope he makes it, I thought; can you get arrested for drunk walking? I wondered. "Famous guide spends night in drunk tank" and sundry other distasteful scenarios motivated my desire to be home sooner than later. We were about halfway to our goal when Edward stopped in his tracks. Dropping my arm and spinning round, his face mere inches from my own, he exclaimed with a kind of astonishment that usually only comes with a moment of sudden and profound insight, "If I'd had one more beer, *I'd be drunk*!" Having gathered all my self-control, I managed, I think, to paste an "oh-my-word-really?" look on my face and we continued staggering home, arm in arm, until arriving at the driveway. Then we saw Cindy. She was sitting on the cement steps at the side of the house and looking uncomfortable. What's wrong with this picture? our beer-soaked brains wondered. Realization dawned as Edward took a few more steps toward Cindy and then stopped. He slapped both hands down on his front pockets, swung around abruptly to face me and barked with considerable gruffness, "Do you have the keys?" "No," I responded, shrugging.

Around to the back of the house we went, quietly, like thieves in the night. Down on all fours, Edward managed to jimmy one of the basement window locks. The windows were small, hinged on the bottom, and opened inward. Immediately Edward started shimmying in on his belly but quickly re-emerged, saying he wasn't tall enough, and commanded, "Donna, you go." I was not much taller than he, but moved quickly to obey, because there was no consideration of discussion when Edward gave a command. At any rate, I had just got both legs parallel to the floor when he broke the still of the night with a bellow, "Don't lean on the window." Any relatively short person who has tried to climb in a basement window without leaning on it knows this is not an easy task, at least without the ability to levitate. Somehow I managed to get one foot onto the plush chair where I could balance my weight, and while pushing hard on my forearms, was able to avoid leaning on the window. After I proceeded upstairs to open the door for the others, all was well that ended well.

The next morning, we woke to hear an ominous crunching sound coming from the next room, quickly followed by an alarming crash. We both started to a sitting position and a moment later a sheepish Edward came into the room and explained, "Well, I locked myself out again, and I leaned on the window..." Of course, he could have pounded on our window to be let in, but he no doubt wanted to prove to himself that he could climb in without leaning on the window, which he couldn't. It was an apology of sorts.

Usually evenings did not end at the pub. At ten o'clock precisely it was hot chocolate and donut time. We would proceed to the kitchen at Edward's direction. Standing at the counter, we would first put pure cocoa and sugar – precisely measured – into our mugs. A little evaporated milk from a can was added to the dry mixture. Then we would stir, round and round with the seriousness of chemists in a laboratory. No lumps were allowed. It had to be a completely smooth paste. Edward would inspect each mug until we got it right. I can still hear the rhythmic *clink, clink, clink* that seemed to go on interminably. Finally, this task accomplished to the required standard, boiling water would be added, followed by more stirring. At last we would sit contemplatively, or telling stories, drinking our hot chocolate and eating donuts, which were always crescent-shaped with sugar sprinkled on them. They were usually a little stale, so it was advisable to dunk them.

Sometimes, late in the evening, with Edward puffing on his pipe and looking thoughtful, we would sit together so quietly that the ticking of the wooden wall clock was the only sound to be heard. It was a stark contrast to our own home environment – music blaring, television propagandizing – always some sort of noise. Wouldn't it be lovely to hear the rhythmic ticking of a clock in my own home? I mused. By eleven or so, this wind-down ritual was over when Edward stood up and said, "Well, goodnight," and off to bed we went.

Our basement room offered privacy, in a manner of speaking, and was a good big space for sorting gear. Everything could easily be spread out on the floor while we agonized over what to take and what not to take on a trip. Edward was always in favour of us carrying as little as possible and would smile at our anxious deliberations, making suggestions which confounded the dictate of carrying as little as possible. "Do you have a pair of thick gloves?" "Don't forget a little extra grub." And he would frequently examine the sundry (and sometimes embarrassing) items scattered about. Once our gear was stowed and the packs leaned up against the wall, Edward would sneak downstairs to check on them. Maybe "sneaking" is not a fair description of his intentions, but we never saw him go down into the basement with the intention of hefting our packs. The hefting part, unbeknownst to Edward, we did witness more than once. Picking each pack up in turn and holding it for a few seconds, he would utter the pronouncement: "Too heavy!" Invariably he would then mutter something Swiss under his breath. Always, in every case, both of our packs *were* too heavy, which left us with the endless dilemma of what to jettison. The best reassessment we ever got was, "Well, it's not too bad," which was his way of saying "it probably won't break your back."

Sometimes we would try to sneak the packs outside or hide them other places. But somehow he always managed to find them. And so, after packing, we would be sitting in the living room seeking some distraction in a book or writing in our journals, when suddenly he would appear in front of us and exclaim, "Too heavy!"

Since he was probably omniscient, it seemed you could hide nothing from Edward. After climbing two peaks over 11,000 feet in one day, we both had very tender thigh muscles. Cindy, limping painfully down the basement steps, heard him approach. She quickly straightened up and continued walking normally – at least *I* thought she was walking normally. Edward grinned as he walked past and queried, "Sore legs?" Cindy responded with all the dignity she could muster: "A little." As soon as he was out of sight, she gave up the pretence.

Edward had amazingly fit-looking legs – not that he ever paraded about in shorts; that would be disgraceful – except when Cindy and I wore them. Then, doing so looked "cool." But he did wear knicker socks, which showed off his lower legs. Once, seeking commiseration, he took off his socks and rolled up his pant legs to show us his slightly curled-under toes, and told us how sore they were. We murmured sympathies, "Oh yes, how painful they must be," but our eyes were transfixed a little higher – to his very impressive calf muscles. Not to trivialize the sufferings of age. Even though his toes did not look that bad to us, they caused him pain when he crammed his feet into old leather hobnail boots to accompany us on glacier trips. When he would gingerly remove his socks at the end of such outings, his feet could be raw, blistered and bleeding. We had great sympathy for him, and if anything his never-give-up attitude gave us more perspective on the struggles and adjustments older people generally face. His body was becoming more of a challenge for him, but in all the important ways he was the same Edward he had always been, and he was not going to let any opportunity for adventure pass him by, even if he had sore feet along with miscellaneous aches and pains for his efforts.

Reminiscing on a lazy day at Lake Louise, but looking around quickly to see if anyone might overhear him, he said, speaking softly, "You know, I was out in the water one day up to here (he gestured toward his hips), bathing, and, uh, I looked up, and a little distance down there," he said, pointing, "was a woman sitting on a rock. I looked at her and she didn't budge. I realized after a moment or two she was *sketching* me," he added, in a shocked voice. He went on to say that he made a hasty retreat. Cindy and I did not retreat but sat musing. Who, with any talent for life drawing, could have resisted the temptation to sketch such a fine subject? What had become of the artist's sketches? we wondered. Were they sold in some trendy New York art gallery? We found it amusing to think that the walls of some Fifth Avenue apartment might be graced with drawings of Edward's torso.

"They put me in a skirt," Edward once quipped provocatively. He had our attention. It turned out he wore the skirt in a skiing scene, as the stand-in for silent film star Alma Rubens.* *The Valley of Silent Men* was filmed at Banff. Shortly before its release in 1922, Edward was quoted by a newspaper reporter as having said about Rubens, "She's the pluckiest girl I ever met."[137] In addition to Edward skiing in drag, the film featured Ms. Rubens in several dramatic scenarios, including crawling up Mount Rundle. She was also filmed inside a crevasse. Edward personally selected the crevasse and then lowered Ms. Rubens into it. The director, Frank Borzage,

* (1897–1931).

was worried about low light on the glacier while shooting the crevasse scene, but Edward reassured him that the light conditions would produce dramatic contrast effects. When Borzage still seemed skeptical, Edward asked him why he had not taken "tests" to ascertain the quality of the footage. Apparently, the film company had not brought equipment to develop film, so Edward offered him the use of his own darkroom. The director took him up on the offer and was delighted with the quality of the tests. Edward was equally delighted to be remunerated by Hollywood for the use of his root cellar.

Edward had always been interviewed for newspaper articles. Later in life he had more spare time but being interviewed became more of an annoyance for him than it had been in the past, and he was not always fully aware of the purpose for which his words would be used. Statements were taken out of context; too much was assumed from a few quips; and some things that were said in confidence appeared in print. Freed from social constraints by the privilege of age, he was blunt at times. And old grudges could suddenly erupt, in the company of some who did not know the context for a remark. Nevertheless, he still maintained a sense of personal propriety. What was said to a group of guides, for example, was not meant for all ears. He would have been mortified to find that some of these stories had spread beyond those he had confided in, or that generalizations had been made from them. At times, he may have said more than he should have, motivated by loneliness and the recognition that he was no longer centre stage in the mountain world. So many of the old-timers were gone, and with them the history they had shared together.

In a letter to Thorington, in his own hand when he was approaching 80, Edward wrote: "It is a long time since you came to the Rockies; so many of the Old Climbers do not come to Canada anymore and I miss them..."[138] Rallying, he went on to detail his plans for the summer, including summiting Mount Temple!

To his credit, he railed against his limitations but did not become bitter. And as his letter to Thorington shows, he did his best to continue setting goals for himself and to enjoy whatever mountain activities he was capable of achieving. While ardently wishing he could take us out on big climbs himself, he gained vicarious satisfaction from our achievements, as he did in the achievements of all those he was fond of.

One charming exchange that shows the intensity of his involvement in others' climbing activities took place between my parents and Edward on the day we had left to climb Mount Victoria on a two-day trip. We were to stay overnight at Abbot Pass Hut and climb the mountain the following day.

Edward: Oh, they'll have a *beautiful* trip to go to Abbot's Pass.

Mike: I hope it's good tomorrow.

Edward: I only hope that he [the guide] doesn't decide to go up Victoria today. [*sounding as*

*if the idea had just occurred to him, and also
becoming dismayed]*

Pat: That would be too much.

Edward: You know those damn young fellas,
they overdo it. What was it, six o'clock in the
morning? [*referring to when we were meeting
the guide*]

Mike: At Wapta.

Edward: That seems to me fishy, six o'clock at
Wapta...
[*calculating the time involved, thinking out
loud*]
Well, he has to go over to Louise; he has to
walk around Louise to get up to the Plain of
Six Glaciers and Abbot's Pass. Well, they could
be up there now...
[*it was about noon when this conversation took
place, and he was right: we were*]
What would they do all afternoon? That
fella – I'll bet he's going to climb Victoria this
afternoon.

Pat [*sounding nervous*]: Think so?

Edward [*responding emphatically*]: That's what I
think.

Mike: I don't think Donna will let him.

Edward [*curtly*]: I hope not.

Mike: If she's tired at all, or Cindy, she won't let him. Donna is very firm; they won't push Donna around.

Pat: Yeah, because that's –

Edward [*interrupting, his speech becoming more pressured*]: Because I don't know him truly. I haven't climbed with him.

Mike [*attempting to reassure him*]: Donna has a mind of her own; she won't let him push her around.

Edward [*still distracted and pondering the prospect of climbing the mountain in one day, continuing to muse out loud*]: Then it would be late in the evening before they get down to O'Hara. If they go around Huber, it will be ten, eleven o'clock at night. Galloping climbing [*an evaluation spat out with disgust*].

Pat: That's no fun; you don't enjoy it.

Edward: I could have done that as a young lad, but I never did it. I believe in going an hour or two, taking it easy and looking around. They don't do that anymore. [*to Mike*]: It's just to say "I've been there." There's no more pleasure. That's the way they climb today; wear themselves out. I wouldn't be a damn bit surprised.

Pat [*softly*]: Wowie.

Edward [*persisting*]: Instead of making two days, go do the whole thing in one. It can be done, alright, if you race.

Pat [*weakly*]: Yeah.

Edward: I told the girls last night, be sure and stay in Abbot Pass Hut overnight so that you can look out through the windows. You get beautiful sunsets over Glacier there.

Pat: And the stars are so nice at night – it's beautiful.

Edward: If they make two days, it's all right.

[*Later that night...*]

Pat: What time do we leave in the morning?

[*They were all going to Louise in hopes of seeing us climbing; a discussion of departure times ensued.*]

Edward: We go right away to the telescope. First thing.
[*some minutes later, having managed to calm himself down*]
They won't sleep much up there in the hut. They'll be too excited.
[*sounding softer now*] I'm damn glad they went.[139]

We did not find out until after he died that the summer after Cindy and I made this climb, Edward had bragged to an interviewer: "Some of my best friends – girls, young girls that I taught when they were babies, going over those high passes. Last year they, the two girls... I got them to climb Mount Victoria last year and Mount Huber."[140]

Edward was frequently kept awake the night before our climbs by excitement and worry. Unfortunately the latter also caused him stomach aches.

There were other, less abstract things that gave *us* stomach aches. Edward did not really cook much in his lifetime, and after Martha died he was faced with this daunting task. Edward used to wax nostalgic from time to time about some of his childhood favourites. *Rösti*, a very simple Swiss dish – in other ethnic terms, rather akin to a giant latke with cheese – was something he craved, and I wonder now, with the clarity of retrospection, why we did not offer to at least try to prepare some for him.

Often we accompanied him to the grocery store, where he would wander aimlessly like some other older-generation Europeans I have known, finally to settle on something he could clearly identify, like "smokies." Smoked, yes (well, maybe), but unlike the meat he cured himself in the old days, now filled with goodness knows what additional ingredients. Also, like some others of his generation, he did not comprehend that refrigeration – or even canning, for that matter – did not render foods edible in perpetuity.

Edward having said with some excitement that he had purchased something special for our dinner, we almost collapsed in a mutual heap when we opened the fridge and discerned that the surprise – pork chops – had a decidedly green tinge and had been purchased well in advance of our visit. We left them for a few days, but then made a decision to just throw them out; we would defend our position that they had seen better days and face the inevitable wrath. Even with our having replaced the delicacy, the ensuing scene was not an especially pleasant one.

Culinary challenges were not always confined to home. As a special treat, we were taken out to a "Chinese and western" cafe for "flapjacks." Cindy and I have never been truly dedicated consumers of pancakes, so we were alarmed when Edward cheerfully ordered "full stacks!" We knew he was meaning to give us something special, but we groaned inwardly, wondering how we would meet the challenge. Unfortunately there was nothing about these particular cakes that was unusual. They were like North American pancakes in cafes everywhere. That is to say they were anemic-looking processed-flour discs as large as dinner plates. We suspected they also contained preservatives that could, in certain sensitive subjects, crack open the "doors of perception" just a bit. However, fearing Edward's crestfallen face if we failed to indulge with a vigour commensurate with the honour, we always settled down to the serious (and somewhat painful) business of making good work of it. I do not think we fooled him.

We were waiting for Seppi to call. Edward wanted us to climb Bugaboo Spire. We had never been to the Bugaboos before; the name itself should have been somewhat forewarning. But we had seen photos of the spires – smooth, clean-looking and sharp, projecting from a vast expanse of ice like randomly erupted granite teeth. When Conrad Kain, Edward and others had descended on the area in 1916, there was great debate about what to call it. According to Conrad, Edward suggested "Aiguilles…, as the spires resemble the aiguilles of Chamonix even more than Mount Assiniboine duplicates the Matterhorn."[141] However, when climbing one of the spires for the first time, Conrad came to a tricky gendarme which he referred to as a bugaboo. The name stuck.

A warm, sunny day with a cloudless sky ended Edward's patience and spurred him to action. "You should go to the Bugaboos today." We stared at him blankly and he added, "I'll go with you." He gave us instructions as to what to pack and then made the phone call. It was a short call, fairly non-specific, and went something like this: "I'm leaving with the girls for the Bugaboos. Meet us there."

Edward had no car by then, so I drove. A scuffle almost ensued when Edward pushed past Cindy and climbed into the back of the car before she had a chance to react. There was no seat in the back. Only a carpeted bench with no seat belt. We both tried to persuade him to move to the passenger seat, but he stubbornly refused. Sitting forward, arms resting on his knees and hands folded, he stared ahead and shook his head "no." Although I really felt as if I were committing elder abuse, I climbed into the driver's seat and headed south. Then came the difficult part: about 50 kilometres of gravel road. In a pristine sports car, it was beyond tedious. From time to time I looked back at him; there was no danger of going off the road at the speeds we were travelling, and each time he said, "I'm okay."

Our first view, which was breathtaking, was of Snowpatch, named for the obvious reason. We parked the car in front of Bugaboo Lodge. Built by the Austrian-Canadian mountain guide and entrepreneur Hans Gmoser, Bugaboo was the first in what became a string of lodges in his pioneering heli-ski operation, Canadian Mountain Holidays.

Edward thought we should visit the lodge, which, although "rustic," seemed very grand to us. Soon Edward was swarmed by admirers, including Hans, and we were given a heaping plate of food, which was welcome, as we still had an arduous three-hour hike with a 2,300-foot elevation gain (about 700 metres) to reach our destination: Boulder Camp, or the Kain Hut. This is a tough hike for a relatively fit young person. It's quite exposed to the sun, ladder climbing is required, and on that day it was scorching hot. Edward, of course, handled the hike well, but he grumbled about the grade, which he found unnecessarily steep. In other words, he felt the trail was badly engineered. Arriving at a similarly steep rock slab, with the hut looming above it, our eyes widened as Edward, carrying a substantial pack, quickly scrambled up on it, having to use his hands as well as his feet. While he could have walked around the slab, it was the equivalent of a "dramatic entrance."

Having staked out claims in the sleeping loft, we waited – anxiously. Much to our delight, Seppi did answer

Edward's summons, arriving in the wee hours of the morning. Not long afterward we headed up the glacier, using headlamps, to Rucksack Pass. This was an appellation Edward had given to the col between Snowpatch and Bugaboo spires because, having ascended it with a client, the latter suddenly realized he had left his pack at the bottom of the pass. One wonders how he could not have noticed there was no weight on his back. He must have been distracted by the view and maybe by amazement at what he was doing. At any rate, while the client stayed put, Edward went back down, muttering, retrieved the pack and trudged back up again. From Rucksack Pass, they started up the ridge and so did we.

There were some steeper sections on the spire itself, and we found the granite a bit challenging in big leather boots, especially because this was our first encounter with this type of rock. Being high up on the ridge had a decidedly airy feel. And soon, like moles, we popped out above a bank of clouds to a startling world dominated by the alluring face of Howser Spire. Then came the bugaboo. Examining it as we awaited our turn, we could see it certainly seemed to have ambiguous toeholds. Best not to think. How we traversed it I do not remember, but I do recall the impressive drop-off. Not much later, with the hut we had left that morning now some 3,000 feet (900 metres) below us, we were revelling in the exhilaration of sitting atop this beautiful spire.

Seppi yodelled several messages to his fellow guides as we climbed down from the summit. After a number of inspirational rappels, we were back on the glacier again.

Edward, who had spent the day on the glacier (with his ice axe, of course), rushed to congratulate us, beaming with pride and excitement. Someone took a photo of Cindy, Edward and me in front of the hut. It was the only mountaineering photograph Edward kept in his living room.

Seppi needed to leave the Bugaboos that very night, in a totally sleep-deprived state. Cindy and I, with our 91-year-old mentor, walked out the next day. We were as light as air.

Back in the world of quotidian activities, Edward liked to do little things for us and forgave us all our lapses in duty, which were many. Everyone knows that upon arriving home from an outing, one immediately sets about the business of cleaning and sorting gear. Be that as it may, Edward found the boots we had left in a shamefully muddy state, and while we were out he cleaned them and applied waterproofing. When we next saw them, all four, clean and shining, were standing at attention, heels up against the foundation of the house.

Efforts to repay kindnesses felt unsuccessful. Once, in my attempt to trim the front hedge, which stretched across the property to the driveway, Edward quickly figured out what was happening and appeared at my side, just as I had begun clipping. Without a word spoken between us, he proceeded to point to every errant and uneven twig in the whole shrub. I clipped, he supervised. Gardening was never meant to be quite this irksome, but Edward was frustratingly perfectionist in everything he did.

Cindy and I had barely arrived in Golden from Los

Angeles and were feeling wobbly after three days of road racing, but Edward was already giving us our commission. Gazing intently into our faces, and with a mixture of gravity and excitement in his voice, he said, "This year I want you to climb Tupper." It was as if a great honour had been bestowed upon us and we smiled self-consciously. Although always flattered by his annual plans for us, we were acutely aware that he was living vicariously in our literal footsteps.

We knew that Mount Tupper was in Rogers Pass. We had gazed at the peak from the safe and civilized perspective of the road many times. But this mountain was different than other mountain mandates we had been given. It was one of Edward's 100-plus first ascents and thus was extra special for us as well as for him. He had climbed Mount Tupper on July 2, 1906, as a very young man, in the company of his cousin Gottfried Feuz and a German client, Wolfgang Köhler.

Edward had promised to show us his first-ascent photos and tell us about the route after dinner that evening. The black and white images carefully pasted into the black-paged album were a good pictorial representation of the climb, but we were not entirely cheered by viewing them. There was decided trepidation at hearing: "And here is the hand-traverse; it will make you smile." Seeing Köhler, arms stiff, inching along on his palms with his feet dangling over the cliff edge, did not exactly defuse anxiety. Still, it was one of those special moments that bound us to a past we had never known but with which we grew to feel a curious familiarity.

That dark summer morning, it seemed particularly cold standing in the driveway of Edward's house as we waited for Seppi to arrive. He was late. It turned out he had had trouble rising due to having imbibed too much the previous evening. Such are the foibles of youth. But as this day was filled with great expectations, we did not feel any sympathy for Seppi's plight, grumpily cramming ourselves, along with our gear, into his two-seater. More than an hour later, after an uncomfortable and largely silent drive, we arrived at our starting point. As we extricated ourselves from the cramped car, the air was damp, the sky still dark.

Using our ice axes as walking sticks, we felt the metal in our hands send cold tendrils through our bodies. With a slight shudder we descended into the trees at the trailhead; it felt as if we were entering a mysterious cave. After a few strides we began moving steadily uphill. Cindy was feeling excitement accompanied by some fleeting worrisome thoughts, but since I was a less efficient morning person myself, I chose a totally unconscious attitude to accompany the steep trail. We were silent for most of the preliminary approach and finally the sun began filtering through the trees. We were warmer and so were our moods, as by this time we were quite cheerfully enjoying the lingering sweetness of wild strawberries on our tongues. Then, properly fortified with a second breakfast of hard-boiled eggs and oatcakes, we forged on toward our goal. Once we reached the rock, we climbed with confident efficiency. It was as if we had been there before…

Meanwhile, across the valley, grinding up the steep Avalanche Crest trail, a 3,500-foot (1070-metre) elevation gain described as "a climber's access route which is rugged and relentless,"[142] the now 93-year-old Edward, hoping to catch a glimpse of us climbing his peak, led our parents determinedly toward his own goal.

CHAPTER 10

EDWARD'S GIRLS

In the summer of 1980, Cindy and I were, as usual, with Edward, who by then was 95 years old. We did not hire a guide that summer, because we were feeling impecunious. Among other adventures, Edward sent us off to Bow Glacier, where we spent four and a half hours chopping steps in the ice above the hut on the way to St. Nicholas Peak, other climbers virtually strolling by us in their crampons. We stopped just short of the summit, for safety reasons as I recall, but we were proud of what we had done. We spent the night at Bow Hut, where one unfortunate bunkmate who was suffering from giardia dissuaded us from drinking the water. When torrential rains, which started early in the evening, had not let up by noon the next day, we decided to leave. With visibility so poor we were barely able to see the trail at all, we cautiously made our way down to our starting point at Bow Lake.

On the following day, Edward led us on our usual three-hour recovery walk around town. We found ourselves at the airport. He reached the edge of the runway, intent on crossing, but there were small planes on the descent for landing. They were far enough away that Edward could not see them, but close enough to pose a real hazard. When we told Edward very emphatically that he *had* to wait, he thought we were being unduly cautious. Nevertheless, we insisted and he waited. Grudgingly. The planes quickly loomed large before us, vindicating our judgment in the matter. Immediately after they landed, Edward carried on with his agenda of crossing the runway. We scampered to keep up with him, fervently hoping we were not going to be hit by the next plane coming in. Keeping our eyes focused straight ahead so we could not see anyone trying to wave us off, we walked on with some perturbation, having quickly grasped the fact that runways are truly wide. We suspected Edward was an experienced runway crosser, but this was the first one we had ever experienced on foot, and with every step we took, over what seemed like an endless distance, we anticipated sirens.

On the other side of the runway there was, not surprisingly in retrospect, barbed wire. Wordlessly and without missing a step, Edward hopped on the lower strand of wire, gripping the top strand with both hands. He got one foot up on the middle wire, but it was too wobbly for him to climb over. No doubt frustrated by what he thought should have been a simple manoeuvre, he gave up the attempt, hit the ground with surprising alacrity and began wriggling under the fence. Glancing at each other in alarm, Cindy and I simultaneously grabbed the lower wire and hauled it up just in time. I managed to continue holding the wire up while Cindy crawled under. Then I climbed the fence, but right next to a metal post, where it was not so wobbly and there was a firm handhold.

Back at home we fell into our usual routine. Edward would leave all the especially interesting mail he had received during the year out on the dining room table so we could read it. Seated around the table, he puffed on his pipe while Cindy and I read. In a month or so I would be off in pursuit of an advanced degree, in Manitoba – on the bald-headed prairie as Edward referred to it. I glanced up to find him gazing at me mournfully. He caught my eye, sighed deeply and uttered only one word, "Winnipeg." He was not the only older friend who did not understand why I had to go *there*. It was so far from home and away from them. All Edward could think was that there are no mountains there. He had chugged away from the prairies' desolate flatness long ago. He knew.

After a brief discussion, it was agreed that Cindy should leave as soon as possible. She climbed into her aging Land Cruiser and drove with determination. Unlocking the door of the house, she stepped inside. It was silent. There was no familiar soft ticking. No heartbeat except her own, now thumping. This she might have expected, but she saw nothing. Nothing except bare, uninspired walls, now looking dingy. No familiar yellow Formica-topped kitchen table. No neatly stacked newspapers or empty blue Edgeworth tobacco tins in the closet. There were no mundane things. All that remained was emptiness. Her eyes brimming with tears, she walked from empty room to empty room, seeking proof. She seized upon a discarded old pipe. It was something – a tangible connection to our old friend – who had been here living and breathing just days before, but now was gone.

It is never easy to lose someone you love, even when they are 96 years old and have lived a full, satisfying life – miraculously without any real illness – a charmed existence, really. Still, greedy for more time with him, we had all secretly hoped he would live to celebrate his 100th birthday.

To cope with our grief, we decided to paint the house. It needed restoring and so did we. Besides, it was something tangible that could help us feel productive and useful; something that we could alter, that we could control – a little gift, as it were. It a was gift we could not have given him when he was alive, because we would have been thought to be wasting precious time we could have spent up in the hills instead of down in the valley labouring. We arrived in May, about a month after his death. The paint from our uncle's factory in Montreal was delivered to Golden by the CPR. We picked it up at the train station, the same one where Edward had arrived with his young family almost 70 years earlier.

We took the job seriously. Standing on the small roof of the sunroom – heavy sanders in our hands – we took breaks to gaze at the familiar hills around us. There was not much talking while we worked; we wanted to do a job that would have made Edward proud. Absorbed in our own thoughts, we knew what we had lost – a dear friend and a proud papa. We were grateful for all the adventures we had had with him and all we had learned and the romantic heritage we had come to share.

After each long day working in the sun, we retired to sleeping bags on the hard floor. Sitting with our backs up against the bare wall, as we had no chairs or any other furniture, we drank hot chocolate and ate slightly stale crescent-shaped donuts as we had done every other summer. Sharing memories of Edward, we felt a little of his presence still with us in the house and could imagine him smiling at our reminiscences.

Later that summer, we returned to the Bugaboos to climb Howser Spire – our special climb that year for Edward. It was a peak he had been close to making a first ascent on in 1916, but bad weather had prevented him from getting to the summit. It seemed like a good choice and we could almost see him rushing toward us, excited about the prospect of our climbing another granite spire and wanting to tell us all about it. Sadly, there were no new experiences with Edward to be had. The old ones were tucked deep down inside the cockles of our hearts. The two of us made another special trip into the mountains, to hold our own memorial service. Among the words we recited was an excerpt from the writings of John Muir we thought Edward would like:

> Climb the mountains and get their good tidings. Nature's peace will flow into you as sunshine flows into trees. The winds will blow their own freshness into you, and the storms their energy, while cares will drop off like autumn leaves.[143]

Always seeking the mountains' good tidings. This was the essence of Edward's life; that and a boundless enthusiasm for sharing those good tidings with others. He was, as he put it, simply crazy for mountains, and his compulsion to experience them, each time anew, endured to the very end. As it happened, he was born in an adventurous and romantic era filled with fascinating characters, all acting out various portions of their life trajectories in an awe-inspiring place. How could it have not been enchanting?

Perhaps romance is an outdated concept in an era of wanting to do more, go higher, faster, longer or better than others, but I hope not. Climbing is more than physical ability – prowess, agility, skill. It is also more than mental attitude – toughness, temerity, focus. One does not need to go the highest or the farthest or to be the fastest to have a satisfying mountain life, although these things are achievements which bring their own accolades. And if this sort of achievement has an element of romance, the more the better. Finding beauty in the ordinary and everyday and in appreciating those who have gone before us, romance is to be found with every step one takes in the mountains, if only even in a figurative sense. Those lucky enough to take the literal steps know – even when some of those steps are laden with apprehension, discomfort or even excruciating fatigue – that this is all part of the process, part of the immediacy of being, which Edward knew forges strong human bonds among one's mountain companions.

Most people find that climbing itself focuses attention.

All extraneous data drifts away and each moment is truly experienced. And I am sure this is part of what many find satisfying about mountaineering and climbing. But to truly find enchantment, there also needs to be passion. This means not just obsession but also subjective feelings of excitement, a sparkle in the eye and a glowing visage – an expectation of the extraordinary. Without passion we can do any number of things blankly and by rote and might as well be counting the number of widgets we assembled at the factory that day. As Edward would say, "What pleasure is there in that?" And if we go to summits only so we can say we've been there, as Edward feared some people might, we would have missed the good tidings. What a shame that would be if it were true.

How Edward did the things he did in his old age – with us as well as with others – always astounded us. Now, decades after his passing, memories of Edward have at times seemed like a distant dream, pleasant but wrapped in gauze and dimly remembered. We questioned ourselves. Did all of this really happen? And more importantly, could we have been so fortunate to have experienced even a little of the enchantment that so many before us enjoyed? We became somewhat unanchored, like orphans. Then, one day, seemingly out of the blue, Seppi smiled knowingly and said, "You were always Edward's girls." And that settled it. With one simple statement, there were no more questions.

It was a plan conceived in the late fall of 2005 with much enthusiasm but also much apprehension. Cindy had not climbed since a very unpleasant incident five or six years earlier. Descending a mountain in the Cascades, she had slipped on a scree-covered ledge and flown over the edge. Thankfully they were roped, but Cindy swung into the mountain with considerable force. She then spent an excruciatingly uncomfortable and sleepless night in a tent. The consequences of her slip turned out to be two cracked ribs. But subtler than ribs, which heal eventually, her confidence had been shaken and she did not really acknowledge the extent of repressed anxiety this incident had engendered. She just did not find herself with the prospect of putting herself in precipitous places again. That is, until now.

I began by appealing to her sense of heritage and applied not so subtle psychological pressure: "It would mean so much. I know you can do it. Edward would *want* you to do it." Finally Cindy agreed, but in the interim I injured my knee. There was an anxiety for our plans welling up in me that I did my best to grimly ignore. In the late spring came the test – several multi-pitch climbs followed by in-door climbing and lots of hiking of increasing intensity. My knee was weak but holding up and Cindy was steadily improving her strength and endurance.

By mid-June, in addition to our own internal fretting and concerns, we were still waiting for the third member of our party to accept our invitation. Now pretty much desperate with anxiety, I wrote an e-mail imploring him to accept. Finally, at the eleventh hour, a message on my voicemail: "Donna, this is Seppi Renner, call me…" At hearing the familiar voice, I found myself smiling in a moment of déjà vu. Immediately after returning Seppi's call, I phoned Cindy. Before she even had a chance to say anything but "hello," I blurted out, "He said yes!" Cindy responded in a similarly restrained manner.

Now we could relax. Or could we? There was, after all, the weather. For months we had been discussing wardrobe, supplies and getting used to new boots. I knew with certainty Cindy could get up the mountain, especially now that we had the security of Seppi's participation, and I was determined to get up the thing if I had to crawl to do it. But weather was not a matter of willpower and good planning. From here on out it was up to chance. The beginning of July is fairly early for a climb in the Selkirks. The *Selkirks*, not some big peak in an exotic land. Not a first ascent. Not even a particularly hard climb. So, what could generate such excitement? For us, it was an anniversary.

As we arrived at Rogers Pass, in another little yellow car, I thought of Wolfgang Köhler's words: "I was astonished at the beautiful wild form of the mountain, ..."[144] There it was, not looking so wild, more like a welcoming old friend, and it seemed that the weather would be fine.

For this trip, we had chosen to stay overnight in relative luxury only minutes from the trailhead. We were subdued that evening – but the anticipation was palpable. The three of us moved around the small hotel room with a coordinated efficiency, readying gear and sandwiches, performing all the nervous rituals that accompany such an adventure, and then tucked into our respective beds.

Edward, Gottfried and Wolfgang had slept in a small

log hut up near the meadow. For them, "The night was wonderfully beautiful, a cloudless sky and brilliant moonlight." We overslept. Startled, we fairly flew to the trailhead and began the upward grind at 5:30 a.m. There was no talking on the trail. It was steep. We were late and chatter is not what we were used to on an approach. Instead, Seppi, Cindy and I were each lost in our own thoughts of doubt and hope, focused solely on getting up the trail. This reunion, 28 years after the three of us had climbed Mount Tupper together, was for Edward.

Again we were walking in his footsteps and in those of all the many adventurers who had gone before us. We could not help but feel that these mountains were infused with their spirits, as if their journeys had somehow left fleeting but perceptible traces in the atmosphere.

Our first task was to hike only 1.7 miles, but gaining 2,400 feet in that distance (732 metres in 2.7 kilometres), negotiating an average grade of 28 per cent. I spent more energy than I should have, due to pausing for photos and then dashing to catch up with the other two. Our first glimpse of Tupper was through the trees as the sun was rising. It stirred the heart, but excitement was tempered by the fact that we were still a long way from the mountain. Finally, two hours later, we arrived at alpine meadows and were greeted by pink and white heather and, amidst patches of snow, carpets of yellow avalanche lilies. From here, it is as Wolfgang says, "always up and then down again. We had innumerable gullies and streams to cross, until we reached the ridge… We rested a little and then started on again…"

Seppi, Cindy and I finally arrived at the glacier, crossed it, and then scrambled up the rocky ridge. Two and a half hours after we had arrived in the meadow below, it was time to rope up. After all these years the three of us were actually climbing together again. Over and over again Seppi exclaimed, "Edward, Edward," and we knew what this meant. Memories of Edward flooded our senses as we climbed the chimney. Cindy and I flashed back to the small black and white photos we had been shown the night before our first climb on Tupper. It seemed like only yesterday that we had experienced Edward's excitement that we would go where he had gone. We imagined the original three comrades on their way to achieving the first ascent of this mountain *100 years before*, and it felt like we were sharing in their exhilaration.

Finally, as with Edward, Gottfried and Wolfgang,

> We stepped over one sharp knife-edged ridge, "tight-rope dancing" we called it, and with a loud hurrah reached the summit.
> "This is really the top," said Edouard. And so we got on to the beautiful broad summit... During the whole way we had the most beautiful views.

Although happy too, I felt a lump in my throat as I surveyed all the peaks that had meant so much to our friend, absent from these mountains for over 25 years but never far from our fondest thoughts.

Able to reveal my surprise at last, I whipped out the bottle of champagne I had hauled up the mountain in my pack and presented it to Seppi, who, much to my disappointment, looked alarmed. Relief spread over his face as he realized the celebratory bottle contained no potential for inebriation. Later he explained that he wondered how we would get down if we drank all that champagne. So, with our glasses in hand, we toasted our friend Edward and his two comrades and ourselves. I remarked that we should have worn hobnail boots, to add a more historically authentic touch to our ascent, but in response received only silent glares.

Upon reaching the summit of Mount Tupper for the very first time – the mountain A.O. Wheeler thought no one could climb – Edward, Gottfried and Wolfgang "built, in three-quarters of an hour, a big stone-man... which could be seen from the railway by the naked eye." After our celebratory summit luncheon Seppi reached into the very same cairn. Pulling out the summit register, he commented that we should use a whole page, given the special nature of the occasion. Carefully smoothing the page and then handing the book to me, he and Cindy looked on with hopeful anticipation. A wave of panic flooded over me. With all the preparations and thought that had gone into our trip, I had somewhat forgotten about the summit register. The written document. The link to mountain heritage and posterity. The pressure was on. I went blank, but somehow words flowed anyway, as they usually do for students sitting a final exam. What I wrote I am not sure, but I guess it was adequate because the other two looked happy and Cindy said it brought tears to her eyes.

As had Edward, Gottfried and Wolfgang, the three of

us then "began the descent in very good humor." And finally, our centennial climb was at an end.

I leave the last sentiment to Wolfgang: "Would that many could see and experience the joy of this beautiful mountain as I have done. To my dear guides I give my best thanks..."

Above the fray, far from the petty concerns of life, the wind blows. An eagle soars. We touch rock again and smile, knowing we will always be Edward's girls.

NOTES

CHAPTER 2: EDWARD

1. William L. Putnam, *The Great Glacier and Its House* (New York: The American Alpine Club, 1982), 203.
2. Georgia Engelhard, "Mountain Man," Whyte Museum of the Canadian Rockies (WMCR), Feuz Family Biofile, periodical title unknown (date unknown), 84.
3. A.O. Wheeler, "Behind the Asulkan and Donkin Passes," *Appalachia* 10, no. 2 (1903): 131.

CHAPTER 3: HOW IT ALL BEGAN

4. Alexander Rechsteiner, "Homesick for the Mountains," October 8, 2019, Swiss National Museum Blog, https://blog.nationalmuseum.ch/en/2019/09/homesick-for-the-mountains/.
5. Rechsteiner, "Homesick for the Mountains."
6. Pierre Berton, *The Last Spike* (Toronto: Anchor Canada), 1.
7. Berton, 335.
8. Eventually, the Rogers Pass portion of track was abandoned after 58 people were killed in an avalanche in 1910 (see Berton). The solution was the five-mile-long Connaught Tunnel under Mount Macdonald. It is an interesting point that although rail travel here had been possible since 1885, the Trans-Canada Highway portion through Rogers Pass was not completed until 1962.
9. See John Snow, *These Mountains are our Sacred Places: The Story of the Stoney People* (Calgary: Fifth House, 2005).

10. The topic of treaties with Indigenous peoples in Canada is extremely complex and far beyond the scope of this book and of my own expertise. Readers who wish to learn more should be wary of written histories which exclude oral traditions of Indigenous peoples.

11. Quoted from H.A. Dempsey, "The Fearsome Firewagons," in *The CPR West: The Iron Road and the Making of a Nation*, edited by H.A. Dempsey (Vancouver: Douglas & McIntyre, 1984), 57.

12. See Walter Wilcox, *The Rockies of Canada* (New York: G.P. Putnam's Sons, 1916).

13. Alison Griffith and Gerry Wingenback, "Interview with Edward Feuz Jr., 1977," WMCR, Archives General File (S8).

14. Mary T.S. Schäffer, "Untrodden Ways," *Canadian Alpine Journal* 1, no. 2 (1908): 289.

15. Of course, not all Indigenous peoples converted to Christianity, the point being that the acceptance of dominant-society norms did not confer equality.

16. H.A. Dempsey noted that a few Stoneys had worked assisting railway survey crews. E.J. Hart's *Trains, Parks and Tourists* (Banff: EJH Literary Enterprises, 2000) mentions that Stoneys acted as guides in 1894 and built pony trails to Lake Agnes. That was also the year when the annual event Banff Indian Days began. Some Indigenous people continued to lead pony treks and various individuals were CPR employees, but these were the exception rather than the rule.

17. See Diccon Bewes, *Slow Train to Switzerland* (London: Nicholas Brealey Publishing, 2014).

18. CPR advertisement, *Canadian Alpine Journal* 2 (1910): unpaginated.

19. CPR advertisement, *Canadian Alpine Journal* 13 (1923): unpaginated.

20. L.S. Amery, "Speech to the English Alpine Club on June 7, 1910," *The Alpine Journal* 25 (1910-1911): 293.

21. See A.O. Wheeler, *The Selkirk Range*, vol. 1, 319.

22. William Putnam, *The Great Glacier and Its House* (New York: American Alpine Club, 1982), 47.

23. Quoted by J.M. Thorington in an obituary of Edward Feuz Sr., *American Alpine Journal* 5, no. 3 (1945): 416.

24. Glacier House Scrapbook, 1899, 28, WMCR, Glacier House Hotel fonds (M262).

25. Glacier House Scrapbook, L. Rich, August 11, 1907, 28.

26. See Jackie Morris, *Trackside Guide to CP Rail* (Revelstoke, BC: Friends of Mount Revelstoke and Glacier, 1993).

27. Lyle Brown, "Interview with Edward Feuz Jr., 1967," WMCR, Canadian Broadcasting Corporation fonds, S7/4; 1 & 2.

28. From a note by H. Worsfold, dated July 21, 1908, in the Glacier House Scrapbook, WMCR, unpaginated photocopy. On July 19, 1908, Worsfold, along with Jean Parker (the daughter of Elizabeth Parker), made the second ascent of Mount Tupper, guided by Edward and his father.

29. William Putnam, *A Climber's Guide to the Interior Ranges of British Columbia – North* (1975).

30. F.V. Longstaff, "The Story of the Swiss Guides in Canada," *Canadian Alpine Journal* 28 (1942–1943), and Longstaff, "The Swiss Guides in Canada: Further Notes," *Canadian Alpine Journal* 29 (1944–1945).

31. All quotes from Edward's *Führer-Buch* are from photocopies held by the Whyte Museum of the Canadian Rockies (WMCR), Edward Feuz fonds (M93/2).

32. C.P. and A.F. Kitchel, Glacier House Scrapbook, August 23, 1906, WMCR, unpaginated photocopy.

33. Information provided by Sepp Renner.

34. Ethel Johns, "A Graduating Climb," *Canadian Alpine Journal* 2, no. 2 (1910): 159.

35. See Elizabeth Parker, "Gossip About a Few Mountaineering Classics," *Canadian Alpine Journal* 12 (1922).

36. A.O. Wheeler, "Rogers Pass at the Summit of the Selkirks," *Canadian Alpine Journal* 17, no. 1 (1928): 51.

37. This was a common assessment. For example, Jon Whyte and Carol Harmon quote C. Henry Warren wondering, in 1926, "if tourists notice how very like a prison it is": *Lake Louise: A Diamond in the Wilderness (Banff: Altitude Publishing, 1982)*, 39.

38. *Führer-Buch.*

39. See Lyle Brown, "Interview with Edward Feuz Jr., 1967," WMCR, Canadian Broadcasting Corporation fonds (S7/4; 1 & 2).

40. Ibid.

41. Unsigned interview with Edward Feuz, *Boston Herald*, August 19, 1937, 2, WMCR, Edward Feuz fonds (M93/5).

42. Kate Gardiner, "A Climbing Trip to the Freshfield Group and Some Other Ascents," *Canadian Alpine Journal* 27, no. 1 (1939): 46.

43. Kate Gardiner, "Letter to J. Monroe Thorington, September 29, 1939," WMCR (M106/102).

44. Georgia Engelhard, "Mountain Man," unknown periodical, WMCR, Feuz Family Biofile (date unknown), 84.

45. The dedication from W.L. Putnam in *A Climber's Guide to the Interior Ranges of British Columbia – North*, published in 1975, reads: "Respectfully dedicated by an admiring follower to the most famous name in Canadian mountaineering, Edward Feuz Jr., whose undimmed spirit takes him still to the heights he taught us to reach."

CHAPTER 4: HOW WE CAME TO SHARE THE ENCHANTMENT

46. There really is nothing new under the sun. On a trip to the Freshfields, J.M. Thorington, Howard Palmer and Edward found boulders. "Some are as big as a bungalow and afford amusing climbs. The largest of all on the ice was ascended by Edward, who built a little cairn on top."

    J. Monroe Thorington, *The Glittering Mountains of Canada* (Philadelphia: John W. Lea, 1925), 39.

    Edward also was very fond of climbing pinnacles, but as these were not mountains, he did not consider them important enough to warrant making a record of which ones he had climbed. David Jones, in his guidebook *Rockies Central*, found some evidence suggesting that Edward might have climbed the Grand Sentinel (a very nice pillar indeed) sometime between 1916 and 1920.

47. Bruce West, "End of an Era," *The Globe and Mail*, August 6, 1965, 29.

CHAPTER 5: FEUZ HAUS

48. L.S. Amery, *Days of Fresh Air: Reminiscences of Outdoor Life* (London: Hutchinson's Universal Book Club, 1940), 210.

49. "Well-known Alpine guide is dead at age 85. He spent twenty years exploring the Canadian Rockies, where his three sons are still carrying on the tradition," *The New York Times*, June 13, 1944. WMCR, Edward Feuz fonds (M93/1).

50. Howard Palmer, *Mountaineering and Exploration in the Selkirks: A Record of Pioneer Work Among the Canadian Alps, 1908–1912* (New York: G.P. Putnam's Sons, 1914).

51. According to her daughter, Alice, until Elise moved out of the village and established her own network of friends, her life was hard. Martha confirmed that there had been friction in her relationship with Elise.

52. See Diccon Bewes, *Slow Train to Switzerland* (London: Nicholas Brealey, 2014).

53. An estimate from the latter part of the 19th century indicated that 30 feet of snow fell each winter at the Illecillewaet Glacier in the Selkirks; see Berton, 1971.

54. Jean Feuz in personal communication with the author.

55. Henry Hall, "The First Ascent of Mt. French," *Canadian Alpine Journal* 12 (1922).

56. This story was told to me by my father, who was staying with the guides at the time of the incident. Waking up to a rifle shot would have been frightening, but it would have been easy for Mike to dismiss the event as humorous once he realized what was happening. For the guides, however, it would have brought to mind Christian Häsler Sr.'s suicide. By the time of this incident, the latter's son had already died.

57. See *Calgary Herald*, December 23, 1974 (page number unknown).

58. Quotes are from letters in the Edward Feuz fonds, WMCR (M93/5).

59. Georgia Engelhard, "Mountain Man," unknown periodical (unknown date), 84.

60. Maryalice Harvey Stewart, "Interview with Edward Feuz Jr., 1974," WMCR (S1/115).

CHAPTER: 6 HOW THEY DID IT

61. E.J. Hart, *Jimmy Simpson: Legend of the Rockies* (Rocky Mountain Books, 2009).

62. Mary Vaux, "Camping in the Canadian Rockies," *Canadian Alpine Journal* (1907), 68.

63. Maryalice Harvey Stewart, "Interview with Jim Boyce, Pat Brewster and Edward Feuz," 1976, WMCR (S1/120).

64. Stewart interview, 1976.

65. Mary Vaux, "Camping...," 69.

66. W.D. Wilcox, *The Rockies of Canada* (New York: G.P. Putnam's Sons, 1909), 153–154.

67. Stewart interview, 1976.

68. A.O. Wheeler and Elizabeth Parker, *The Selkirk Mountains: A Guide for Mountain Climbers* and *Pilgrims* (Winnipeg: Stovel Co., 1912), 4.

69. Stewart interview, 1976

70. J.W.A. Hickson, "Mountaineering in the Canadian Alps, 1906–1925," *Appalachia* 16, no. 3 (1926): 243.

71. W.E. Stone, "Amateur Climbing," *Canadian Alpine Journal* 11 (1920): 1–8.

72. A.H. MacCarthy, "The First Ascent of Mt. Eon and its Fatality," *Canadian Alpine Journal* 12 (1921, 1922): 16.

73. Longstaff, "The Story of the Swiss Guides in Canada" *Canadian Alpine Journal* 28 (1942–1943): 196.

74. Ibid.

75. MacCarthy, "The First Ascent of Mt. Eon...," 25.

76. J. Monroe Thorington, *The Glittering Mountains of Canada: Old Trails of the Rockies* (Philadelphia: John W. Lea, 1925), 40.

77. Howard Palmer, *Mountaineering and Exploration in the Selkirks* (New York: G.P. Putnam's Sons, 1914), 317.

78. Ibid., 325.

79. Kenneth A. Henderson, *The American Alpine Club's Handbook of American Mountaineering* (Boston: Houghton Mifflin Co., 1942), 24.

80. J.W.A. Hickson, "Two First Ascents in the Rockies," *Canadian Alpine Journal* 3 (1911): 44.

81. Ibid., 47.

82. Phil Dowling, "Interview with Edward Feuz Jr., 1978," WMCR, Archives General File (S8/accn. 3004).

83. Hickson, "Two First Ascents...", 47.

84. Thorington, *The Glittering Mountains...*, 44.

85. J.W.A. Hickson, "The Ascent of Pinnacle Mountain and Second Ascent of Mount Deltaform," *Canadian Alpine Journal* 2, no. 2 (1910): 52.

86. W.S. Jackson, "The First Ascent of the Central Peak of Mt. Bagheera," *Canadian Alpine Journal* 1 (1907): 103.

87. See Dowling interview, 1978.

88. All quotes by Rudi Gertsch are from personal communication with the author.

89. Lyle Brown, Interview with Edward Feuz Jr., 1967, WMCR (S1/63).

90. Hickson, "The Ascent of Pinnacle Mountain...", 56.

91. W. Osgood Field, "Mountaineering on the Columbia Icefield," *Appalachia* 16 (1924–1926): 148.

CHAPTER 7: READING THE SIGNS

92. Howard Palmer, "Travel and Ascents Among the Highest Canadian Rockies," *Appalachia* 16, no. 3 (1926): 258.

93. J. Monroe Thorington, *The Glittering Mountains of Canada* (Philadelphia: John W. Lea, 1925), 102.

94. Peter Ross, "The Apprenticeship of Bruno Engler," *Mountain Heritage Magazine: The Journal of Rocky Mountain Life and History* 2, no. 2 (1999): 20.

95. Joseph Hickson, "Around Bow Pass, the Saskatchewan River and Cathedral Crags," *Canadian Alpine Journal* 14 (1924): 13.

96. See Phyllis Rose, *Alfred Stieglitz: Taking Pictures, Making Painters* (New Haven: Yale University Press, 2019).

97. See Jeffrey Hogrefe, *O'Keeffe: The Life of an American Legend* (New York: Bantam Books, 1992).

98. Ethel Johns, "A Graduating Climb," *Canadian Alpine Journal* 2, no. 2 (1910): 162.

99. Lillian Gest in conversation with the author.

100. Lulu Grau, "Sept. 5, 1904," in *This Wild Spirit: Women in the Rocky Mountains of Canada*, edited by Colleen Skidmore (Edmonton: University of Alberta Press, 2006), 188.

101. Howard Palmer, *Mountaineering and Exploration in the Selkirks* (New York: G.P. Putnam's Sons, 1914), 320.

102. Ibid., 321.

103. Unknown article title and author, *Boston Herald*, August 19, 1937, 2. WMCR (M93).

104. *Führer-Buch* note, September 6, 1941.

105. Bruno Engler's story of "the dandy" and all direct quotes in this section are from his book *A Mountain Life* (Canmore, AB: Alpine Club of Canada, 1996), 42–46.

106. See Griffith and Wingenbach interview cited in chapter 3 at note 13.

107. Hickson, "The Ascent of Pinnacle Mountain…," 49, 50.

108. Hickson, "Mountaineering in the Canadian Alps: 1906–1925," *Appalachia* 16, no. 3 (1926): 233.

109. See Lyle Brown, Interview with Edward Feuz Jr., 1970, WMCR (S1/63).

110. Hickson, "Mountaineering in the Canadian Alps," 232.

111. See Dowling interview, 1978.

112. *Canadian Alpine Journal* 1, no. 2 (1908): 329.

113. Winston Churchill, *My Early Life: A Roving Commission* (London & Glasgow: Fontana Books, 1972), 25–26.

114. Ibid., 26.

115. Susan Leslie, ed., *In the Western Mountains: Early Mountaineering in British Columbia*, BC Provincial Archives Aural History Program, *Sound Heritage* 8, no. 4 (1980), 11.

116. Quotes from the climbs with Amery were taken from the Lyle Brown interview (WMCR); see also Susan Leslie, ed., *In the Western Mountains*.

117. Letter from L.S. Amery to H.F. Mathews, General Manager Western [CPR] Hotels, Edward Feuz fonds, WMCR (M93/5).

118. *Führer-Buch* note, September 6, 1941.

119. Hickson, "Mountaineering in the Canadian Alps," 246.

120. *Führer-Buch* note, August 9, 1951.

121. Anecdote recounted by Edward in conversation with the author.

CHAPTER 8: SNAPSHOTS

122. Quotes from Edward on his last ascent of Mt. Temple are from an interview with Sue Davies in 1970, WMCR (S1/63).

123. See Hickson's note, *Canadian Alpine Journal* 4 (1912): 143.

124. Hickson, "The Ascent of Pinnacle Mountain…," 52.

125. Lillian Gest, *History of Moraine Lake* (s.l., s.n., 1970), 25.

126. Martha Feuz, letter to J. Monroe Thorington, WMCR (M106/102).

127. No author identified, *Canadian Alpine Journal* 4 (1912): · 144.

128. "82-Year-Old Guide Leads Hike Over Pass," August 4, 1966, WMCR, Feuz Family Biofile.

129. See Edward's *Führer-Buch*.

130. Brian Patton and Bart Robinson, *The Canadian Rockies Trail Guide: A Hiker's Manual* (Banff: Summerthought, 1971), 179.

131. G.W. Culver, "The First Traverse of Mount Victoria," *Canadian Alpine Journal* 2, no. 2 (1910): 94.

132. See William L. Putnam, *The Great Glacier and Its House* (New York: American Alpine Club, 1982).

133. Charles Fay, in the Glacier House Scrapbook, WMCR, 39.

134. See Putnam, *The Great Glacier and Its House*, 143.

135. Marleen Macquoil, "The Last of the Original Rocky Mountaineers," October 1977, WMCR, Feuz Biofile.

CHAPTER 9: LIFE WITH EDWARD

136. John Barnard Gest, Gest Family Papers 1861–1936, University of Pennsylvania Archives.

137. Quoted from an article entitled "Famous Guide Piloted Photoplayer," WMCR (M93/5).

138. Edward Feuz, "Letter to J. Monroe Thorington, April 2, 1964," WMCR (M106/102).

139. Stephen Collection (audio).

140. Alison Griffith and Gerry Wingenbach, Interview with Edward Feuz Jr., 1977, WMCR (S8).

141. Conrad Kain, "Reminiscences of Seven Summers in Canada," *American Alpine Journal* 1, no. 3 (1931): 292.

142. Patton & Robinson, *The Canadian Rockies Trail Guide...*, 84.

CHAPTER 10: EDWARD'S GIRLS

143. John Muir, *Wilderness Essays* (Salt Lake City: Peregrine Smith Books, 1987), 199.

144. All ensuing quotes so attributed are from Wolfgang Köhler, "Ascent of Mount Tupper," *Canadian Alpine Journal* 2, no. 1 (1909): 31–36.

BIBLIOGRAPHY

Amery, L.S. *Days of Fresh Air*. London: Hutchinson & Co., 1940.

———. *In the Rain and the Sun*. London: Hutchinson & Co., 1946.

———. Letter to H.R. Matthews (n.d.). Whyte Museum of the Canadian Rockies, Edward Feuz fonds (M93/5).

———. "Speech to the English Alpine Club." *The Alpine Journal* 25 (1910): 293.

Bernet, Peter. "Lachen im Winter, weinem im Sommer." *Jungfrau Zeitung*, March 4, 2011.

Berton, Pierre. *The Last Spike: The Great Railway 1881–1885*. Toronto: Anchor Canada, 1971.

Bewes, Diccon. *Slow Train to Switzerland*. London: Nicholas Brealey, 2014.

———. *Swiss Watching: Inside the Land of Milk and Money*. London: Nicholas Brealey, 2012

Burks, Jan. "The Naming of the Lyells." *Canadian Alpine Journal* 58 (1975): 43–44.

Burpee, Lawrence J. *Among the Canadian Alps*. Toronto: Bell & Cockburn, 1914.

Brown, Lyle. Interview with Edward Feuz Jr., 1967. Whyte Museum of the Canadian Rockies, Canadian Broadcasting Corporation fonds, S7/4 (1), (2).

Cavell, Edward. *Legacy in Ice: The Vaux Family and the Canadian Alps*. Banff: The Peter and Catherine Whyte Foundation, 1983.

Calgary Herald. "82-Year-Old Guide Leads Hike Over Pass,"

August 4, 1966. Whyte Museum of the Canadian Rockies, Feuz Family Biofile.

Churchill, Winston S. *My Early Life: A Roving Commission.* London & Glasgow: Fontana Books, 1972.

Culver, G.W. "The First Traverse of Mount Victoria." *Canadian Alpine Journal* 2, no. 2 (1910): 92–94.

Davies, Sue Corless. Interview with Edward Feuz Jr., 1970. Whyte Museum Oral History Programme (S1/63).

Dempsey, H.A. "The Fearsome Firewagons." In *The CPR West: The Iron Road and the Making of a Nation*, edited by H.A. Dempsey, 54–69. Vancouver: Douglas & McIntyre, 1984.

Dowling, Phil. Interview with Edward Feuz Jr., 1978. Whyte Museum of the Canadian Rockies, Archives General File, (S8).

Engelhard, Georgia. "Mountain Man: The Photographs of Edward Feuz Jr." (periodical name unknown). Whyte Museum of the Canadian Rockies, Feuz Family Biofile (date unknown): 81–85.

Engler, Bruno. *A Mountain Life: The Stories and Photos of Bruno Engler*, edited by R.W. Sandford. Canmore, AB.: Alpine Club of Canada, 2001.

Feuz, Edward. Whyte Museum of the Canadian Rockies, Edward Feuz fonds (M93/1–7).

———. Letter to J. Monroe Thorington, 1922. Whyte Museum of the Canadian Rockies, J. Monroe Thorington papers and photographic series 1871–1974 (106/120).

———. "Führer-Buch of Edward Feuz Jr." Multiple authors (incomplete photocopy). Whyte Museum of the Canadian Rockies, Edward Feuz fonds (M93/2).

Feuz, Ernst. Whyte Museum of the Canadian Rockies, Ernst (Ernest) Feuz fonds (M131).

Feuz, Martha. "Letter to J. Monroe Thorington." Whyte Museum of the Canadian Rockies, (M106/102).

———. "Letter to D.L. Stephen." Stephen Collection.

Field, W. Osgood. "Mountaineering on the Columbia Icefield." *Appalachia* 16, no. 12 (1925): 144–154.

Freeborn, Frank. "A Day on Sir Donald." *Canadian Alpine Journal* 1, no. 2 (1908): 211–215.

Gardiner, Kate. "A Climbing Trip to the Freshfield Group and Some Other Ascents." *Canadian Alpine Journal* 27, no. 1 (1939): 41–46.

———. "Letter to J. Monroe Thorington, September 29, 1939." Whyte Museum of the Canadian Rockies (M106/102).

Gardom, Garde B. "Speech, 1999 Swiss Guide Centennial" [transcript]. Whyte Museum of the Canadian Rockies (01.4/ G17 Pam).

Gest, John Barnard. "Gest Family Papers 1861–1936." University of Pennsylvania Archives.

Gest, Lillian. *History of Moraine Lake*. S.l., s.n., 1970.

Glacier House Scrapbook (numerous authors). Whyte Museum of the Canadian Rockies, Glacier House Hotel fonds (M262).

Grau, Lulu. "Sept. 5, 1904." In *This Wild Spirit: Women in the Rocky Mountains of Canada*, edited by Colleen Skidmore, 187–189. Edmonton: University of Alberta Press, 2006.

Griffith, Alison, and Gerry Wingenbach. Interview with Edward Feuz Jr., 1977. Whyte Museum of the Canadian Rockies, Archives General File (S8).

Hall, Henry. "The First Ascent of Mt. French." *Canadian Alpine Journal* 12 (1922): 38–52.

Hart, E.J. *Trains, Parks and Tourists: The Golden Age of Canadian Travel*. Banff: EJH Literary Enterprises, 2000.

———. *Jimmy Simpson: Legend of the Rockies*. Calgary: Rocky Mountain Books, 2009.

Henderson, Kenneth A. *The American Alpine Club's Handbook of American Mountaineering*. Boston: Houghton Mifflin Co., 1942.

Hickson, Joseph W.A. "A Climbing Trip to the Freshfields Group and Some Other Ascents." *Canadian Alpine Journal* 27 (1939): 39–44.

———. "Around Bow Pass, the Saskatchewan River and Cathedral Crags." *Canadian Alpine Journal* 14 (1924): 1–17.

———. "The Ascent of Mount Moloch." *Canadian Alpine Journal* 9 (1918): 17–31.

———. "The Ascent of Pinnacle Mountain and Second Ascent of Mount Deltaform." *Canadian Alpine Journal* 2, no. 2 (1910): 45–60.

———. "Ascents in the Canadian Rockies – 1926." *Canadian Alpine Journal* 16 (1928): 44–54.

———. "Ascents of Mounts Deltaform and Douglas: Corrigenda." *Canadian Alpine Journal* 4 (1912): 143.

———. "The British and French Military Groups Revisited." *Canadian Alpine Journal* 17 (1928): 39–47.

———. "Experiences in the Canadian Rockies in 1915." *Canadian Alpine Journal* 6 (1916): 33–47.

———. "Mountaineering in the Canadian Alps 1906–1925." *Appalachia* 16, no. 3 (1926): 230–253.

———. "A Mountaineering Trip to the British and French Military and Assiniboine Groups." *Canadian Alpine Journal* 11 (1920): 9–27.

———. "New Climbs in the Canadian Rockies in 1930." *Canadian Alpine Journal* 19 (1931): 33–47.

———. "Notes of a Trip to the Saskatchewan River and Freshfield Glacier." *Canadian Alpine Journal* 6 (1915): 93–98.

————. "Some Climbs in the Canadian Rockies in 1910." *Appalachia* 12 (1911): 226–236.

————. "Travel and Ascents South of Banff." *American Alpine Journal* 1 (1929): 1–6.

————. "Two First Ascents in the Rockies." *Canadian Alpine Journal* 3 (1911): 40–56.

————. "A Visit to the Saskatchewan Valley and Mount Forbes." *Canadian Alpine Journal* 12 (1922): 26–37.

Hind, Robert C. "Edward Feuz 1884–1981." *Canadian Alpine Journal* 65 (1982): 44.

Hogrefe, Jeffrey. *O'Keeffe: The Life of an American Legend.* New York: Bantam Books, 1992.

Jackson, W.S. "The First Ascent of the Central Peak of Mt. Bagheera." *Canadian Alpine Journal* 1 (1907): 100–103.

Jones, David P. *Rockies Central: The Climbers Guide to the Rocky Mountains of Canada*, vol. 2. Squamish, BC: High Col Press, 2015.

Johns, Ethel. "A Graduating Climb." *Canadian Alpine Journal* 2, no. 2 (1910): 158–164.

Kain, Conrad. "Reminiscences of Seven Summers in Canada." *American Alpine Journal* 1, no. 3 (1931): 290–295.

King, Thomas. *The Inconvenient Indian: A Curious Account of Native People in North America.* Toronto: Anchor Canada, 2013.

Köhler, Wolfgang. "Ascent of Mt. Tupper." *Canadian Alpine Journal* 2, no. 1 (1909): 31–36.

Leslie, Susan, ed. *In the Western Mountains: Early Mountaineering in British Columbia."* Victoria: BC Provincial Archives Aural History Program, *Sound Heritage* 8, no. 4 (1980).

Longstaff, F.V. "The Late Christian Hasler (Swiss guide)." *The Daily Colonist* (Victoria, BC), November 17, 1940:

unpaginated. Whyte Museum of the Canadian Rockies (M93/5).

———. "The Story of the Swiss Guides in Canada." *Canadian Alpine Journal* 28 (1942–1943): 189–197.

———. "The Swiss Guides in Canada: Further Notes." *Canadian Alpine Journal* 29 (1944–1945): 49–52.

MacCarthy, A.H. "The First Ascent of Mt. Eon and Its Fatality." *Canadian Alpine Journal* 12 (1921, 1922): 14–25.

Macquoil, Marleen. "The Last of the Original Rocky Mountaineers." Whyte Museum of the Canadian Rockies, Feuz Biofile, October 1977, 6.

Morris, Jackie. *Trackside Guide to CP Rail.* Revelstoke, BC: Friends of Mount Revelstoke and Glacier, 1993.

Morton, Marcus. "Mount French of the British Military Group." *Appalachia* 16, no. 12 (1925): 324–334.

Muir, John. *Wilderness Essays.* Salt Lake City: Peregrine Smith Books, 1987.

Orchard, Imbert. Interview with Edward Feuz Jr., 1964, "Edward Feuz Jr.: Mountain Guide." In *In the Western Mountains: Early Mountaineering in British Columbia*, edited by Susan Leslie, 10–14. Transcript and audio available in Provincial Archives of British Columbia, Victoria: Sound Heritage Series 8, no. 4 (1980): 10–15.

Palmer, Howard. *Mountaineering and Exploration in the Selkirks: A Record of Pioneer Work Among the Canadian Alps, 1908–1912.* New York: G.P. Putnam's Sons, 1914.

———. "Travels and Ascents Among the Highest Canadian Rockies." *Appalachia* 16, no. 3 (1926): 257–277.

Parker, Elizabeth. "Gossip About a Few Mountaineering Classics." *Canadian Alpine Journal* 12 (1922): 133–142.

Patton, Brian, and Bart Robinson. *The Canadian Rockies Trail Guide: A Hiker's Manual.* Banff: Summerthought, 1971.

Putnam, William Lowell. *A Climber's Guide to the Interior Ranges of British Columbia – North*. New York: American Alpine Club, 1975.

———. *The Great Glacier and Its House: The Story of the First Center of Alpinism in North America, 1885–1925*. New York: American Alpine Club, 1982.

Rechsteiner, Alexander. "Homesick for the Mountains," October 8, 2019. Swiss National Museum Blog. https://blog.national museum.ch/en/2019/09/homesick-for-the-mountains/.

Rose, Phyllis. *Alfred Stieglitz: Taking Pictures, Making Painters*. New Haven and London: Yale University Press, 2019.

Ross, Peter. "The Apprenticeship of Bruno Engler." Interview with Bruno Engler. *Mountain Heritage Magazine: The Journal of Rocky Mountain Life and History* 2, no. 2 (1999): 16–22.

Sandford, Robert W. *The Canadian Alps: The History of Mountaineering in Canada*. Banff: Altitude Publishing, 1990.

Schäffer, Mary T.S. "Untrodden Ways." *Canadian Alpine Journal* 1, no. 2 (1908): 288–294.

Shepler, Dwight. "How to Know People – Climb Mountains with Them." *Boston Herald*, August 29, 1937. Whyte Museum of the Canadian Rockies, Edward Feuz fonds (M93/5).

Skidmore, Colleen, ed. *This Wild Spirit: Women in the Rocky Mountains of Canada*. Edmonton: University of Alberta Press, 2006.

Snow, John. *These Mountains are Our Sacred Places: The Story of the Stoney People*. Calgary: Fifth House, 2005.

Stewart, Maryalice Harvey. Interview with Edward Feuz, 1974. Whyte Museum of the Canadian Rockies, Oral History Programme (S1/115).

———. Interview with Jim Boyce, Pat Brewster and Edward Feuz, 1976. Whyte Museum of the Canadian Rockies, Oral History Programme (S1/120).

Stone, W.E. "Amateur Climbing." *Canadian Alpine Journal* 11 (1920): 1–8.

Thorington, J. Monroe. "Edward Feuz Sr. (1859–1944)." *American Alpine Journal* 5, no. 3 (1945): 416–417.

———. "The Freshfield Group." *Canadian Alpine Journal* 13 (1923): 64–69.

———. *The Glittering Mountains of Canada*. Philadelphia: John W. Lea, 1925. Reprinted with a foreword by Robert William Sandford. Calgary: Rocky Mountain Books, 2012.

Vaux, Mary. "Camping in the Canadian Rockies." *Canadian Alpine Journal* 1 (1907): 67–70.

West, Bruce. "End of an Era." *The Globe and Mail*, August 6, 1965: 29. Whyte Museum of the Canadian Rockies, Edward Feuz fonds (M93/5).

Wheeler, A.O. "Behind the Asulkan and Donkin Passes." *Appalachia* 10, no. 2 (1903): 123–135.

———. "Rogers Pass at the Summit of the Selkirks." *Canadian Alpine Journal* 17, no. 1 (1928): 47–58.

———. *The Selkirk Range*. Ottawa: Government Printing Bureau, 1905 (2 vols.).

Wheeler, A.O., and Elizabeth Parker. *The Selkirk Mountains: A Guide for Mountain Climbers and Pilgrims*. Winnipeg: Stovel Co., 1912.

Whyte, Catherine. "Interview with Edward Feuz Jr., March 5, 1967." Whyte Museum of the Canadian Rockies, Peter and Catherine Whyte fonds (S37/7).

Whyte, Jon, and Carol Harmon. *Lake Louise: A Diamond in the Wilderness*. Banff: Altitude Publishing, 1982.

Wilcox, Walter Dwight. *The Rockies of Canada*. 3rd ed. New York: G.P. Putnam's Sons, 1909. Reprinted with a foreword by Neil Wedin. Mountain Classics Collection. Calgary: Rocky Mountain Books, 2008.

INDEX

Note: Page numbers in italics refer to photographs.

Broadcasting
Corporation), 220–21

Chalet Ultima, Switzerland,
96

Chamberlain, Neville, 60

Chateau Lake Louise, 37,
51–56, 94–95, *149*, 182,
243–44

Chester, T. E., 58

Christian Peak, 235–36

Churchill, Winston, 194–95

Clarke, Charles, 38

Cochrane, J. M., 45

Columbia Icefields, 114

Columbia Mountains, 41
See also Selkirk
Mountains

Columbia River, 41, 71, 77

Cook, Thomas, 36

Cooper, H., 42n

Craigellachie, British
Columbia, 30

Cromwell, Tony (Eaton), 74,
96, *155*

Culver, G. W., 223–24

D

Davies, Jim, 220

Dempsey, H. A., 32–33

Devils Thumb Mountain, 16,
165, 181

E

Eagle Peak, *145*

Eagle's Eyrie, 227

Edelweiss Village, *150*, 245
building of, 71–72
daily life in, 76, 78,
80–87
See also Canadian Pacific
Railway (CPR)

Edward Peak, 235–36

Edwin (Îyârhe Nakoda
man), 33

Eiffel Peak, 206

Eiger Mountain, 23

Emerald Lake, 41, 93, 109

Engelhard, Agnes Stieglitz,
182

Engelhard, George, 182

Engelhard, Georgia, 96, 100,
155, *164*, 182–83, 208, 224

England, 40, 49, 60

Engler, Bruno, 56–57, 178,
180, 187–90, 220–21, 235

Ernest Peak, 235–36

F

Fairview Mountain, 243

Fay, Charles E., 38, *160*, 229

Feuz, Alfred (E.'s brother),
24n

Feuz, Alice (E.'s niece). *See*
Pollard, Alice

J

Jackson, W. S., 133–34

Janet (E.'s German
Shepherd), 101, *158*

Jimmy (marmot), 214–15

Johns, Ethel, 49–50, 183–84

Jorimann, Christian, 49n

Jungfrau Mountain, 23, 28,
144

K

Kain, Conrad, 57, 120–21,
193, 265

Kain Hut, *171*, 266

Kaufman, Christian, 42n,
207

Kaufman, Hans, 42n, 207

Kicking Horse Canyon, 41

Kicking Horse Pass, 41

Kicking Horse River, 41

Kingman, Henry, 219

Kitchel, Allan, 45–46

Kitchel, Cornelius, 45–46

Köhler, Wolfgang, 269,
281–85

L

Laggan Station, Alberta, 41,
52

Lake Agnes, 33, *165*

Lake Agnes teahouse, 96

Lake Louise, 18, 33, 36, 41,

42n, 49n, 60, 64, 75, 101,
132, *149*, *158*, *159*

    Chateau Lake Louise, 37,
51–56, 94–95, *149*, 182,
243–44

    Guide House, 91, 92, 96,
156

    Plain of Six Glaciers
teahouse, 54, 89–91,
138, *154*, 187, 209

Lake Oesa, 220, 221, 222–23

Lake O'Hara, 93, 112n, 132,
184, 216, 219–20, 222–23,
228

Lake O'Hara Lodge, 216

Larch Valley, 204, 205

Lausanne, Switzerland,
28–30

Lindsay, Lennox, 120

Linn, John, 205–6

London, Ontario, 50

Lugano, Switzerland, 180

Lüscher, Hans, 243–44

M

MacCarthy, A. H., 43, 57,
119–21

Macdonald, John A., 30, 32

Mallory, George, 22

Matterhorn Mountain,
50–51, 229

Mendelssohn, Felix, 23